OUR TIME AFTER A WHILE
Reflections of a Borderline Baby Boomer

Lloyd Billingsley

iUniverse, Inc.
New York   Bloomington

Our Time after a While
Reflections of a Borderline Baby Boomer

Copyright © 2010 Lloyd Billingsley

iUniverse books may be ordered through booksellers or by contacting:

iUniverse
1663 Liberty Drive
Bloomington, IN 47403
www.iuniverse.com
1-800-Authors (1-800-288-4677)

ISBN: 978-1-4502-0464-4 (pbk)
ISBN: 978-1-4502-0466-8 (cloth)
ISBN: 978-1-4502-0465-1 (ebk)

Printed in the United States of America

iUniverse rev. date: 2/18/2010

As the years pile up, it is strange how one's memories careen back further and further.

—Christopher Plummer*

*From *In Spite of Myself*, Knopf, 2008.

For the Glenwood Public School class of 1963

I was coming around the corner from the Tops Dairy Bar, at the corner of Grand Marais Road and Dominion Boulevard. The place had closed for the day but some of the locals, including Francis "Fats" Reaume, were still hanging out around the side, smoking cigarettes and shooting the breeze, as they did on many a summer evening. These two guys drove up in a black and white 1955 Ford, with loud mufflers and the rear end low to the ground. Nobody knew who they were or where they were from but the passenger told Fats that they were looking for Leonard Bertelli, a strange request.

Leonard was one of the toughest guys in town, maybe the toughest, someone you definitely did not want to mess with. Leonard's very name inspired fear and trembling. Now here was this guy nobody knew wanting to fight him. Fats fielded the request and drove off.

In about 10 minutes Fats came back, not with Leonard, evidently unavailable, but his youngest brother Dickie, who got out of the car while it was still moving and tore into the challenger. I remember the sound of Dickie's fists smashing the guy's face, and that it wasn't much like what you heard in the movies. It was all over in less than a minute. Dickie really hung a job on him, as they used to say. The other guy, the driver and a kind of corner man, made no attempt to intervene and when it was over he didn't want any part of Dickie, who could have done a lot more damage than he did. I don't remember all Dickie said, but he suggested in the strongest terms that if these guys ever showed up again, it would be worse. Maybe Leonard himself would settle the score. The defeated pair drove off but as it happened I saw them again that weekend.

They had picked up a couple of girls, a rather sleazy looking pair I had never seen before, and were parked near Vincent Massey high school. I saw them drive up, four in the car, then it was all below eye level, but there was definitely some strenuous activity going on inside that vehicle, what parkers down by the Detroit River at Heppenstahl's, a name visible on a building across the river, called "watching the submarine races." Back at the Dairy Bar I duly reported to Fats Reaume, whom I occasionally talked to about cars, that I had seen the pair with some girls.

"That's logical," Fats said, with the detachment of a philosopher.

These events took place in 1962, same year as the Cuban Missile Crisis, in Windsor, Ontario, where the vast Great Lakes chain, which includes Lake St. Clair, makes a kind of U-turn, nearly surrounding Essex County with water. From Windsor, one can look north into the continental United States, the only place where it is possible to do so from Canada. The riverfront view serves up the skyline of Detroit, a city with which it shares a rolling heritage, and a lot more. The river and border may divide them, but in some ways they are the same town. Though Windsor calls itself the Rose City, it is really, like Detroit, the motor city, from which "Motown" of course derives. Both are built on cars, on the Canadian side mostly Chrysler cars, as attested by billboards proclaiming WHAT CHRYSLER BUILDS BUILDS WINDSOR.

Ford once built V-8 engines there, such as the 351W or 351 Windsor, and maintained a test track. General Motors produced trim but "Chrysler's," as it is possessively referred to locally, built the whole car. After World War II, they were building lots of them, which required hundreds of "feeder" plants, tool and die shops, stamping outfits like National Auto Radiator, forges such as Great Lakes Forging, trucking companies, railways, and of course labor.

The jobs drew thousands, from everywhere, and many settled in south Windsor, then Sandwich West Township. Roughly speaking, the unofficial boundaries of this "hood," ran from the Third Concession road on the north to Cousineau on the south, though Cabana Road was kind of a de facto boundary, and from Huron Line on the West to Dougall on the east. Not a huge area, to be sure, maybe five square miles, and still opening up at the time, with tracts of woods still standing around the edges.

Rankin Bush, for example, ran from Rankin Blvd. all the way to Huron Line, and was so dense a kid could easily get the feeling he was the first person to prowl the place. Bozo Bush spread north of Third Concession, near the teachers' college, reputedly named, according to Danny Langlois, for a dog named Bozo, who lived at a house on the periphery. This bush was rumored to be the domain of a mysterious "Slingshot Louie" and his gang. Past Dougall Ave. stood Devonshire Bush, spreading nearly all the way to Howard Ave, one of Windsor's main arteries.

During the 1950s and 1960s, this suburban square proved that the phrase "post-war baby boom" was no misnomer. The streets positively teemed with children. I was one of them, but I was not born there. I entered this world in northern Manitoba, where my father, a mechanical engineer, worked in a mine along with two of his brothers. We departed when I was an infant for Cobourg, Ontario, and then Alliance, Ohio, the first place I remember. There my father worked for a conveyor company and I played on coal piles, to the great dismay of my mother. From Alliance we moved to Detroit where my brother Phillip was born, in Henry Ford Hospital.

We lived in a first-floor rental at 2010 Clements, near Davison. In winter a truck would pull up to the place and dump coal into a bin in the basement. I watched my father shovel it into the furnace. There were still streetcars running at that time, and that honking rhythm and blues boomed from every window, the first music I recall with any clarity. I distinctly remember the advent of "Merry Christmas Baby," by Charles Brown, and that most of the people in a nearby park, like some of my playmates, were black, though it meant nothing at the time. One such family would invite me to look at the fish they had caught, still alive and in the sink. It was in Detroit where I fell on the sidewalk and cut myself on a pop bottle, narrowly missing a key vein in the wrist. The scar bears witness. It was also in Detroit where our dentist, in the Penobscot building, took me out of the chair after an extraction and turned me upside down.

My father put his engineering talents to work for the Big Three automakers. He continued to do so when we moved across the river to south Windsor, where I found company in abundance. My fellow baby boomers in that border region, many also born elsewhere, have not been the subject of many books or films about what they did, where they hung out, their schools and teachers, heroes and villains, the particular rules and mores that prevailed, the private dramas in which they took part, the jokes they told, their loves and hates, triumphs and failures. Some years ago I began to think that there ought to be some written record, if for no other reason than to have one. In a sense, the ability to remember demands it, and the time has come, before it all becomes too distant, while some of the landmarks still stand, and while most of us are still around to remember. It's also, I suppose, an act of defiance, an attempt to stop the inexorable march of Time, and a protest against the gradual demolition and disappearance of the world we knew.

Life is lived forward, but understood backward. The present is fleeting, the future uncertain. The past is really all we have for certain. I often can't remember where I put my keys, yet in the middle of a Tuesday afternoon, with deadlines and multiple projects in play, a scene from Curry Park in 1960 will suddenly come to mind with startling clarity. Yes, it's been so long now, as Joe Hinton sang (the song by Willie Nelson) but it seems like it was only yesterday. In fact, sometimes it seems like today. Judging from the emails I get, those I grew up with have the same experience.

Whenever we get together, the stories flow. Many a sentence begins: "Remember when . . ." A look of mischievous glee spreads over faces and the laughter is long and loud. It is as though time has stopped. Some relating the tales thought I should be the official archeologist and scribe. It is true that as a professional writer for most of my adult life I suppose the assignment makes sense. But there is more to it than that.

Readers of Evelyn Waugh's *Brideshead Revisited* will recall that it opens in England during World War II, with home-front soldiers approaching a castle. A corporal, Hooper, breathlessly describes the site, with its lawns, fountain and chapel, to captain Charles Ryder, who listens, as a flood of memories sweeps in.

"You've never seen such a place," Hooper says.

"Yes I have," Ryder says. "I've been there before."

"Well, you've been there before," Hooper says. "You know all about it."

He had been there before. He knew all about it. I grew up in Windsor *et environs*, and also lived in Detroit. I know all about it. In the end, that's the only real qualification. Like Mr. Chips in the James Hilton novel, I want to dredge up the memories and make a book of them. I write not only for those who were there, but for all who grew up in that time, whatever the place. As Motown artist Marvin Gaye said, echoing many a preacher, can I get a witness? It is my belief that great swaths of the experience will be familiar to all of our generation. And there are a lot of us. Those not from the motor cities, or those of a newer generation, may discover some things they didn't know.

For one thing, a radio station in Windsor played a key role in making national figures of artists such as Stevie Wonder, The Four Tops, the Temptations, Dionne Warwick, and the music known as Motown. Elton John, even, owes a great deal to one woman who worked at that station.

For another thing, just as some Americans dodged the draft by coming to Canada, thousands of Canadians joined the U.S. Army specifically to fight in Vietnam. Some did not return, and Windsor is home to a memorial for them. It's down by the river, facing Detroit. A lot of people don't know about it.

I do not write to contribute to any strictly historical or sociological record, though scholarly types and critics of all denominations are welcome to forage, along with all readers of all ages and motives. I made no attempt to formally organize the account by chronology, theme, or subject, which would both falsify my own condition and force the story into a mold. It's more a question of what else than what next. And my purpose is certainly not to produce an autobiography of Lloyd Billingsley – a pretty frightening thought, or maybe a bad joke – though by necessity the story is from my point of view, and can't help being my story. Even so, I know full well that it is also the story of many others, and I tell it with a lot of help from my friends. Oh, yes, a lot of help from my friends.

Memory can fade, like the black-and-white photographs our parents pasted into albums. I may well have some of it wrong, or maybe too black and white. The portraits, as I recall them, may displease some people, but such are the risks of looking back. Doubtless, I would not come off well in a memoir by some members of the old crowd, especially some of the girls. And all, of course, are welcome to fire away at me in print. But even a guy I will call Bernie Muntz, who used to sneak up behind me and grind snow into my face, would find nothing but good will. So would the guys who used to flick wet towels at me in the dressing room at Central Pool, and the lifeguard who shoved me into the fence. Time has worked its healing effect.

Hardly a day goes by when I don't think of my friends, and all that happened back then. So there's a real sense in which I never left at all. I'm like Bob Seger, who lived just across the river in Detroit, and whom we knew about long before anybody in New York or Los Angeles. Like him, I'm still humming a song from 1962. Like him, I remember, I remember. That's what this is about.

And I say to myself, to paraphrase Louis Armstrong, it was a wonderful world, but why keep it to oneself? Why not let everyone backpack with me through that world, if they care to tag along? One can never recapture it all, of course, but who knows what other memories the attempt might dredge up, maybe colorizing some of those black-and-white stills, and making the case for yet a longer account. And who knows what ghosts might come out of the woodwork?

Meanwhile, what follows, though subject to all my limitations, and they are many, is a labor of love. My purpose from the beginning has been simple, to summon that still small voice that says, yes, that's the way it was.

Houses of Commons

As a visit to Ford Malden, the Baby House and other landmarks confirm, the Windsor-Detroit border region boasts a long and colorful history. Here armies marched and Tecumseh held forth. Warships fought it out on Lake Erie during the war of 1812. Here Windsor bootleggers in speedboats tried to outrun American police during Prohibition, apparently with considerable success. As the cenotaph in Jackson Park attests, here Canadian troops departed for Vimy and Dieppe, many never to return. Here from 1939-1941 more than a few Americans came to join the Canadian army, before the United States officially joined the conflict. Here Canadian troops departed for Normandy, and the Lancaster bomber in Jackson Park reminds us of the role our parents played in World War II. Indeed, "What did your dad do in the war?" was a common question. Our fathers did a lot, just as our grandfathers did in World War I, but they didn't care to talk about it much. They took down the German National Socialist regime but were relieved to have survived the conflict and eager to get on with their lives.

Many neighborhoods in Windsor are "wartime houses" but in the post-war boom, our area was still opening up, and almost all the houses were new. The phone prefixes were originally based on "Clearwater," later changed to "Yorktown." Curry, Rankin, and Longfellow were some of the early streets, with others filling in, matching the original streets in Windsor proper. Others, such as Academy Drive, matched local landmarks.

St. Mary's Academy had long stood as the centerpiece of the area, a vast four-story brick structure fronted by a tower with four spires, centered on a soaring chapel, and replete with quoins, cornices, arches and elaborate brickwork, a truly magnificent piece of architecture. It was completed in 1929, a year before the great Penobscot Building that dominates the Detroit skyline, the year of the stock market crash, at a cost of $1 million, when there wasn't much of anything or anybody in the area.

The Academy was our Chartres cathedral, our Notre Dame, our St. Paul's. It looked like it had stood there for centuries and its sheer mass gave the impression that it would still be standing long after everything around it had been reduced to rubble. An institution of the Sisters of the Holy Names, it was formerly downtown, in a smaller but similarly impressive structure that was torn down to make way for the Windsor-Detroit tunnel. Progress and all that.

The grounds of St. Mary's covered at least 20 acres, surrounded by a chain-link fence six feet high, but I never saw the gates closed nor much activity of any kind. Occasionally one would spot a nun, sometimes mocked as "penguins," and I did hear someone call one by name. I cannot recall ever addressing one myself and found them, like the rest of the place, decidedly on the mysterious side.

Whatever activity took place was mostly on the inside, where I never ventured a single time, though others did, for school, music lessons, religious services, and just to look around. We would ride our bikes on the paved road surrounding the building and sometimes grab fruit off the trees. The grounds were peaceful enough, but I always had the sense that I should get out of there, fast. I heard rumors of an angry guard, some old man with a shotgun loaded with rock-salt, but I never saw such a person. The place retained a sense of mystery but with Central Park, a major hangout, right beside it, one couldn't help but investigate.

A grotto that had been at the downtown location was reassembled on the grounds, to the right as you went through the gate. It was built of some kind of volcanic rock, black and very porous, and we would prowl through there along these passageways. One led to this little balcony. Sometimes we would pour out the wax from the candles on our hands, where it hardened and made us look like lepers. I can't recall a single reprimand, something we definitely deserved. So did the kids who would stick lit cigarettes in the mouth of the Virgin Mary statue. I never did that. Even kids sometimes know their limitations.

Our street, McKay, begins at the Detroit River but here all the houses were new, and the street not even paved when we moved in. The one-story brick homes offered three small bedrooms, one bath, and a basement but no garage. For a new house at 3116 McKay, my father and mother, Kenneth Billingsley and Victoria Billingsley, paid in the neighborhood of $11,000. I believe the contractor was Economy Homes and we were the first to live there. Many of my friends were also the first to live in their houses. The places were virtually identical, with the builders not even bothering to reverse the design, though paint, trim and landscaping gave a personal touch. The roof design also showed some variation. On other streets, where Morris Homes and other companies worked, tri-level models prevailed, and these were sometimes reversed. The split-level home was the latest thing, a badge of progress.

The McKay house had hardwood floors which made the hall a convenient bowling alley, for use with these small wooden pins and ball about the size of a cueball. The place also featured a milk chute, about a foot square, by the back door, big enough for a small child to worm his way into the house. Milkmen still ran their routes then, as Bobby Lewis noted in "Tossin' and Turnin,'" a tune from 1961. We used the chute for its intended purpose, and some not intended. On one occasion I used it to shoot at birds with a bb-gun. When I finally hit a sparrow it caused me great distress. I buried the bird in the garden at the back corner of the yard and put up a little cross made of twigs.

The new street was for the most part barren as the Gobi but our place came with an extra, a 50-foot elm tree in the back yard that provided shade for the sandbox our father built. Jimmy Dugal, one of my first friends, used to climb to the highest branches and hang from his knees, which terrified my mother. The tree also served as a refuge for starlings, a kind of black rat with wings, and very noisy. My father, an accomplished archer, once responded to some early morning squawking by shooting the bird right off its perch with a special arrow he called a flu-flu, with spiral feathers. He really nailed that thing and, unlike me with the sparrow, he did not regret it.

In 1939, when he was 15, my father had falsified his age to join the Canadian army and fight Hitler. When booted out for this act, he promptly joined the Merchant Marine, where he was in even more danger. He served the duration of the war. Told after the war he was too late to register for college, he informed some bureaucratic loon, who asked him why he was late, that he had been serving his country for five years and that they better let him in or he would bust up the place. He got in and three years later emerged with his degree in mechanical engineering. He contributed to the design of the tip-cab truck and also worked on the Chevrolet Corvette. We were not wealthy, not by a long shot. But we never lacked for anything and I didn't know anybody who did.

My father stood nearly six-foot-five and bestrode the yard like a colossus. I remember him, with his aviator sunglasses, very stylish for the time, and brow beaded with sweat, digging post holes for the fence, which I would attempt to walk like a tightrope artist, with little success. I helped him and my mother to seed the lawn, which they fertilized with something called Vigoro, stuff that came in yellow bags, purchased from Alpine Nursery on Dougall Ave, near the railyards. They also surrounded the place with shrubs and planted two sunburst locust trees in the front yard, which sloped gently down to the street.

The lawn quickly filled in and cutting it was one of my early tasks, first with a push mower then a Briggs and Stratton power outfit that would get clogged with cuttings and required cleaning out several times during each outing. After cleaning it out I would push the throttle down and rev the thing up. The mower also sliced the tip off my father's shoe on one occasion. With this machine I also earned pocket money cutting the grass of Mrs. Folean, a widow who lived next door, and whose relatives, the Bakers, became friends with my parents. It was only years later I discovered that Mrs. Folean was a Jehovah's Witness. But she never said a thing to me or, as far as I know, to my parents.

After the grass and landscaping filled in, the McKay house became a kind of prop in a game called "anti-i-over." My dad would call out this formula then throw a softball over the house, which we would catch or retrieve. He would also play hide-and-seek with us. For a big man, he was adept at sneaking up on you. I would retaliate by hiding behind the front door and jumping on him when he came home from work in our black 1951 Dodge coupe.

When it was up to us, the choice of game was often British Bulldog, where two opposing teams called out for someone on the other side to come across, and he then had to run the gauntlet. The teachers didn't like it, and neither did parents because you could come home with mud and grass stains on your knees, and maybe a bloody nose. But I suppose it was good training for football. These games, like a lot of our activity, would somehow get organized without any adults.

From our house it didn't take long to reach the Detroit River. But the neighborhood had a waterway of its own.

Across the Creek

About 100 yards from our front door the Grand Marais Ditch flowed parallel to Grand Marais Road. We pronounced both not in the elegant French inflection of CBC announcers but "maris," like Roger Maris, the New York Yankees outfielder, then entering the prime of his career. This artery starts as a natural creek, just where I don't know, but in our neighborhood it was very much a ditch, with the man-made look, though a kind of mother of all ditches, flowing straight as an arrow until it crosses Huron Line. It flowed into a sewage treatment plant of some sort there, and after that the ditch starts to meander like a real creek toward River Canard. I never saw the thing flood its banks, as the name implies, but when the water really drummed down, as it does in Windsor, Canada's bayou country, basements would flood. Then there would be talk of sump pumps and so on.

Tornado warnings would come over radio and television, but one never touched down in our hood, at least not while I was there. Thunderstorms, however, regularly rock the place. My dad showed me how to count off the seconds from a lightning flash to the first clap of thunder. It was one of those childhood discoveries that brings a sense of wonder and delight. So did the fireflies that would swarm on summer nights, when you could see black-and-white televisions through open windows. Not many houses had air conditioning, then for the most part limited to noisy window units that weren't very good.

The fireflies were out in force one night when they had a concert in the parking lot of the IGA store, with a local band playing "Walk Don't Run," by the Ventures. The band played on some kind of trailer. I don't remember the group's name but the musicians were young. It wasn't unusual at the time for 14-year-olds to have a functioning rock-and-roll band.

The banks of the Grand Marais ditch, which usually smelled pretty foul, were cut too steep for play but the ditch did provide a place for a rite of passage. Near the Dominion Boulevard bridge, a gas pipe about one foot in diameter crossed the ditch, about four feet below the level of the street, and an easy 30 feet from bank to bank. This pipe provided a challenge not to be resisted. I made it across sitting down, sliding in increments of inches. In this neighborhood, word spread fast. My mother found out and scolded me. "You crazy kid," she said. But of course I crossed the pipe again. If you stopped in the middle, people in cars would look at you as they crossed the Dominion bridge.

A few kids walked across the pipe with barely a hitch, something I cannot recall ever doing, though I tried on those first few feet, when you still had some bank below. The trick was to step it off at a good pace, but I wasn't up to the task, despite cries of "chicken" from those with superior balance and guts, which can also qualify as folly. Potential crossers did fall in, but I never saw anybody take the plunge, a good 10-foot drop to the water, which was normally only a foot or so deep. I heard stories of boys riding bicycles across the pipe, but never saw anybody do that either. You'd have to be pretty good to pull off that stunt.

Two large vacant lots bordered the ditch at the end of our street, stretching from Curry to Dominion, where the houses took over. They put in a footbridge at the end of McKay but well worn paths crossed these lots, mostly tangled with scrub brush and weeds. A mulberry tree stood in the middle of one, providing a hangout of sorts. Once we found some *Playboy* magazines hidden nearby. Talk about a sense of wonder. To paraphrase Barbra Streisand, mammaries lit the corners of our minds. There was also a mulberry tree on the other side of the ditch right beside the parking lot of the IGA store, which at one time was a Loblaw's store. The joke went around that the heir to the Loblaw fortune was Robert Loblaw, or Bob Loblaw. Say that fast a few times. IGA meant something like International Grocers Alliance but got tagged as "I Grab Apples."

Various pear and apple trees could also be found in empty lots at the edge of housing developments, probably traces from some orchard in the area's agricultural past. The location of these trees was a kind of secret freemasonry. Kids had favorite "climbing trees," some of them in people's front yards. Curry was an older, more treed street, with a little boulevard near the bridge. The corner house, a large two-story brick place, belonged to the Durochers, a common name in Windsor, and featured an excellent climbing tree. One evening I fell out of that tree and broke my right wrist. My father drove me to Hotel Dieu hospital on Ouellette Avenue, where the doctor covered my face with a mask oozing this reeking, stupefying gas, which turned out to be ether. I emerged with a rather cumbersome cast, which soon bore the autographs of my friends. My own writing, always bad enough even with my right hand, became a true scrawl with the left. I remember being shocked at my stick of an arm when they took off the cast but I recovered quickly. Kids are pretty indestructible and we were no exception.

I never actually saw the Durocher family, only their son Tommy, a rather squat boy who was retarded and bore that classic look of bewilderment at the world, an imprint that remains through life. Tommy was of course the butt of many jokes from supposedly normal kids. He wore his pants very high, which prompted Mark Lantz, always quick with a quip, to wonder if Tommy might somehow choke himself.

Fred West, one of the older locals, taught Tommy Durocher to say "damn right!" in response to simple questions such as, "nice day isn't it?" From then on, Tommy would say, "damn right!" as his stock response to everything, including queries about the weather. After pronouncing, he would beam with pride, as though he had just delivered some ringing speech to the city council.

Tommy was a fixture in the neighborhood, though I never saw him farther than Curry Park or Yorktown Square. When he came to the park, I don't recall anyone objecting to his presence. Perhaps it was because everyone was so much alike that the prospect of somebody different was welcome. There was also a feeling that everybody there belonged, that the neighborhood was a kind of family, what a sociologist or church youth worker might call a "sense of community." But Tommy wasn't the only one who was different, or "special."

Johnny Spears, who lived on Rankin Blvd, down by Glenwood School, was a gangly kid, more lucid than Tommy, but far short of erudition. Johnny shuffled around in awkward lurches, often with his hands in his pockets. He was one of those people who thinks he has to hold his face very near to you when he speaks, and capable of a kind of madcap Jerry Lewis humor, much of it unintentional and self-accompanied with a cackling laugh. He blabbed like an auctioneer on speed and would show up at stores and baseball games. He liked to hang around with the Cushmans, Bob and Gord, who lived on the corner of Rankin and Norfolk, and who treated him as a kind of mascot.

Mark Lantz, who wondered if Tommy would choke himself, lived right across from me, at 3109 McKay, and was my age. He had a brother, Danny, the same age as my brother Philip, and Mark's father, Bud, drove trucks in Detroit. Like my father, and many others in Windsor, he crossed the border every day and thought nothing of it. People would sometimes say that they worked "across the creek."

Bud was big on smelt, a kind of oversized freshwater sardine. During the spawning run, these could be scooped out of Lake Erie with buckets. They used to clean the fish with this big pair of scissors. The Lantz family had a black 1958 Ford that Mark would sometimes fire up in the driveway when his parents weren't home. One time he laid rubber and had to take a brush and rub off the tire mark. Bud didn't notice, but he probably suspected that Mark tampered with the car.

Bruce Stibbard lived on Dominion in the house directly behind ours. During a dart game he once missed the target so bad he stuck Mark Lantz right in the thigh. Mr. Stibbard was a short, stocky, angry kind of man with a booming voice. The houses in the hood were well-spaced, with spacious back yards, but some days you could hear Mr. Stibbard yell, "Brucie, how many times have I told you to close the door when you go to the bathroom!" As they say now, too much information. Mr. Stibbard also managed to yank the gearshift out of his 1957 Dodge. My father also bought one of those, a blue "Crusader" model four-door sedan with a V-8 engine and goofy tail fins. Even new it was a piece of junk. He wound up trading it for a 1959 Rambler station wagon, which also had fins and wasn't much of an improvement mechanically. The column shift was a ball joint design that often got stuck in one gear, or in neutral. He eventually replaced it with a floor shift, which I thought was very cool at the time. Like most cars in Windsor, it had a rust problem, which we would call "cancer."

Our street was home to the Silvers, one of the few Jewish families in the area, the Mandells, Shanfields and Novaks among them. The Silvers lived right next to Mike and Kathy Bull, the two children of Roy Bull and Joy Bull. In summer the Silvers put up this big above-ground pool in their back yard and invited all the kids to dive in. That was before they built the pool in Central Park. One really cold day, Mrs. Silver drove several of us to school. I remember her scraping the ice off the windshield, a common activity.

The local climate of freezing wet winters and hot humid summers, with swarms of flies and mosquitoes is something we refugees prefer to forget. Spring and fall were pleasant, bringing the smell of freshly cut grass. I would probably opt for fall as my favorite season in that part of the world. It wasn't full of false promises, like spring, and the leaves turned color, a blaze of glory before a normally gray winter.

Mr. Silver, a man of considerable girth, took care of the green stamps at the N&D grocery store. When you bought things you earned these stamps that could be redeemed for goods. Oddly enough, their official name was S&M Green Stamps. What the letters actually stood for I don't recall. That these letters evoked nary a comment is evidence that, while more hanky panky was going on behind the scenes than one imagined, this was indeed a more innocent time. Mr. Silver gathered vast piles of the canceled stamp books, which he burned in the vacant lot at the end of the street, lest someone retrieve them from the trash and cash them in again.

Ron Silver once found himself in an argument with Paul Adams over gefilte fish, which Paul insisted must be "filleted fish," or didn't exist at all. Paul was not a very subtle kid, and Ronny finally gave up on dietary questions.

The N&D store on Grand Marais was also a hangout of sorts and we got in the habit of sampling the fruit, a practice the clerks did not find amusing. I was in there once with schoolmate and neighbor Larry Roy, who had not taken anything but found one of the clerks in the section staring at him, as though he suspected Larry was about to grab something. Larry looked at the guy and mouthed the words "fuck off," but the clerk got the message, even though by the sound of him he hadn't lived in Canada that long.

"Why for you say fuck off?" he told Larry, who wasn't a tough guy or athletic, but had a lot of moxie. But Larry hadn't expected a response like that and didn't have any comebacks at the time.

The store was the ultimate neighborhood grocery and had been founded by Nick and Dan Budimir, an enterprising local pair of Balkan origins who could often be seen on the premises. These astute businessmen saw fit to expand with the needs of the community. In the early days the front door was on Grand Marais, then after expansion in the late 1950s the doors faced Curry and the parking lot of Yorktown Square. The store sponsored baseball teams and offered N&D jackets. The inventory was the usual fare, some of which no longer exists.

You could buy this margarine, for example, in a plastic sack complete with this little pack of dye, which you worked into the stuff by squeezing it like clay, so the color resembled butter. You had to be careful not to break the bag, which I did once by playing catch with it. Some locals pronounced this material "marjareen" and by rights it should be a long vowel.

You could also buy these things called Flavor Straws or Flavo-Straws. These consisted of a flexible tube full of flavoring. You stuck it in some milk, and the straw imparted a fake strawberry taste. This product was short lived, but spawned a lewd insult. You would hear someone say, "Eat me raw with a Flavor Straw." Something similar happened with cereals.

Many were the same as today, with the Rice Krispies slogan of "snap, crackle, and pop." This motivated a joke about "Post Prostitutes." They don't snap, crackle and pop, just lie at the bottom of the box and bang. You could send away cereal box tops and in return get a submarine or frogman fueled by baking soda, and which you would immediately take on maneuvers in the bathtub. But "box top" was also code for something else. As one joke had it, my girlfriend can't wrestle but you ought to see her box.

One commercial encouraged kids to say "I want my Maypo," for the breakfast gruel that most kids hated, me included, though brown sugar made Maypo and other brands of porridge at least edible. With most kids the slogan rang true that "Sugar Pops are tops."

Hangouts

The N&D was part of a complex at the corner of Grand Marais and Dominion Boulevard that included the Tops Dairy Bar, formerly the Essex Dairy Bar, with a sign shaped like a barrel. The offices of the local weekly, the *Sandwich West Herald*, were also in there, upstairs, but with the door at street level right beside the Dominion Barber Shop. One of the editors was English, with an accent so thick I could hardly understand him.

The other corners of the intersection housed a White Rose gas station, right across from the Dairy Bar; an IGA, or Loblaws, depending on the year; and Christ the King Church. Attached to the IGA were Master Cleaners, Wansbrough's Sport Shop, Pat and Hank's Fish and Chips and, down at the end at the corner of Longfellow, the South Windsor Pharmacy. Around the corner, but part of the same complex, was a shoemaker's shop, run by a rather ornery man with a foreign accent and thick glasses. He used to get angry when you checked to see if stuff was done. He could also prove rather crabby when the shoes were indeed ready for pickup. The complex also hosted Dr. Munholland's office and the South Windsor Barber Shop, later run by a genial fellow named Leo Santamaria, no relation to Mongo. This intersection, therefore, was a spiritual, medical, commercial and social center of our world.

The White Rose station, once operated by Leo Ferri, then by Fred Chalmers, was a popular place to inflate bicycle tires and it had one of those pumps with a crank that spun a set of numbers like those on the gas pumps. A bell dinged off if you cranked it too much. Trouble was, the compressor wasn't always turned on and, no matter what setting, the thing sometimes took air *out* of your tires. Like other stations, the White Rose also had a rubber line that, when crossed, would set off a bell inside, indicating a motorist awaiting service. They didn't like it when you drove over that cord on your bike, but we did.

One of the mechanics was Hank Villancourt, a puffy-faced guy who looked like Broderick Crawford, of *All the Kings's Men* fame, then starring in a television show called "Highway Patrol." Crawford played Dan Mathews and I remember him asking someone, "did a green Chevy coupe come by here?" As for Hank, he seemed to always have a toothpick his mouth, even when smoking. If he had time he would help you fix flats on your bike, but he would warn you about pinching the tube when you put it back together. If you pinched it and then brought it back to him, he would chew you out but usually fix it again anyway if he had the time.

The Dairy Bar had provided a Sunday morning hangout for those who didn't want to go to church. Instead they heard the Reverend Bud Fuller, as the owner came to be known. I recall him as a middle-aged bald guy, an avuncular type and Windsor veteran from way back. Apparently he was also a cop, but I had no clue at the time. Bud liked to talk it up about sports and indeed always seemed to be there on Sunday. But he didn't put up with any mess from the kids, and neither did his partner, Vern, who was older. A teenager named Pete also worked there, along with various part timers.

Along the left side of the Dairy Bar ran a lunch counter outfitted with those stools with the grooved metal trim, and which conveniently spun around. Atop the counter stood several juke-box selectors, five cents a pop, with those metal tabs to flip through the selections. I remember seeing "Petite Fleur" in there, a Sidney Bechet tune, though I didn't know it at the time. There was also Everly Brothers stuff, Little Richard, Elvis, and Chuck Berry, the whole lineup. When I think of the Dairy Bar, the tune that most comes to mind is "Who Put the Bomp?" as the singer, Barry Mann might put it, right to the bottom of my boogety-boogety shoe. Someone always seemed to have it playing on a transistor radio, a status symbol among us, especially if yours had nine transistors, as opposed to, say, six.

These gadgets got free advertising in "Transistor Sister," a tune by Freddy Cannon, I believe, or someone who sounded a lot like him. Freddy also sang "Palisades Park," and "Tallahassee Lassie," about a girl with "a hi-fi chassis." Another tune that seemed to be always playing in the Dairy Bar was "Smoky Places," which laments a young couple's need to hide in shadowy corners, where no one can see their faces. It might have been a local hit because few people remember it. The group, the Corsairs, sounded like the Drifters. So did the Jarmels, who sang "A Little Bit of Soap," another tune that always seemed to be playing around the Dairy Bar.

The Dairy Bar served burgers, fries, milkshakes and such but most customers came for cigarettes, candy, popsicles, and soft drinks, which everyone called "pop." Near the door stood one of those red Coca-Cola machines that dispensed the small bottles. A more general, horizontal-style cooler stored the various brands in rows on metal runners. You slid the bottle to a metal latch, put in a dime and it would open, releasing your drink.

I preferred Fanta, a lemon-lime concoction in a stylish green bottle that had these ribs around the neck. But 2-Way, one of several 7-Up imitators, had its merits. Another favorite was cream soda, this red fluid in a clear bottle, so sweet you could call it sickly. Double Cola, a rival to Coke, came in huge 16-ounce bottles. Vernor's Ginger Ale, a local brand, was also popular. When you would open the bottle, it would fizz, to the point that you would almost have to hold your nose to take a drink. I don't think Faygo Cola, an "old-fashioned root beer," was available in Windsor but we sure knew about it. It was an American product heavily advertised on radio, in a kind of old-fashion western serial, with this Black Bart character.

"Where did he go?" the ads said. "He went for Faaaaaaaygo."

Television carried another ad that still proves useful when verifying anybody's claim to have grown up around Windsor or Detroit:

You're on the right track
To Nine-Mile and Mack
Roy O'Brien trucks and cars
Make your money back.

Roy O'Brien's got them buyin' and buyin'
They come from many miles away
To save themselves a lot of dollars, dollars,
By driving on his way today.

The visual was a cartoon, followed by film footage of someone with an open hand, into which another pressed dollar bills.

Most bottles, meanwhile, were returnable and "picking up pop bottles," provided an introduction to commerce for many in the neighborhood, along with the venerable lemonade stand, cutting lawns, and delivering newspapers. The small bottles were two cents, the big ones five, and for a time there was an intermediate size that brought three cents. You paid one price to drink on the premises and another if you took it away. "Are you going to drink that here?" Bud, Pete or Vern would ask. It was acceptable on these conditions to drink it sitting on the ledge under the front window, as long as you returned the bottle. Call it an early form of recycling.

The Dairy Bar also dispensed candy, including those red licorice strings that were popular and, along with the other junk we ate, kept dentists in business. You could get these "Chunky" chocolates advertised on television by a guy with horn-rimmed glasses who called himself Arnold Stang and spoke in this exaggerated New York accent. Elvis Costello resembles him, and I believe Arnold appeared in a few movies. Eat More chocolate bars were popular for two reasons. They tasted good and you could fold the wrapper so it spelled "Eat Me."

This time was the Age of the Cigarette, for all ages. The Dairy Bar sold candy cigarettes, the ones with about a quarter-inch of red on the end for authenticity, bubble-gum cigars, and those little wax bottles with about one swig of sweet drink inside. Who knows what was in that stuff. Blackballs were a kind of misnomer because they changed color as you sucked on them. All this stuff was "bad for you," as adults would say. That doubtless formed part of its appeal. Most adults smoked heavily, so kids failed to take their warnings seriously.

Hot Rods and Nomads

In pop, candy and ice cream alone the Dairy Bar did a bang-up business, especially after little-league softball games at the Christ the King baseball diamonds, when players and coaches jammed the place. Those baseball cards, which came with those sheets of pink chewing gum, just flew out the door. Kids tore them open to see what big stars they got, such as Warren Spahn, Willie Mays, Whitey Ford, Lou Burdette, Ted Kluzewski, Ernie Banks, Harmon Killebrew, Hank Aaron, Rocky Colavito and so on. The most desirable cards were of Detroit Tigers players such as Al Kaline, Harvey Kuenn, and Norm Cash. One Tigers player, Reno Bertoia, was from Windsor and everybody wanted his card. Reno wasn't a big star, more of a utility player, but he was one of ours and he made the pro ranks, no easy task at any time. You could see some of these very players at Briggs Stadium, as the Tigers' home field was then called, where my father took us several times, once to see the New York Yankees. The presidents of the National and American leagues had cards of their own, but you couldn't give those away.

The Dairy Bar had no air conditioning but a big fan at the back ventilated the place. Toward the back they also had stationed of those machines that tested television tubes. My uncle Ed Cox, who lived across Cabana on Roseland Drive, thought these were bogus and said you could buy 10 new tubes and the machine would tell you seven were no good. I never put his test to the test, but I can testify that the televisions of the day were rather unreliable, and often went haywire in the middle of something you wanted to watch. Someone was always fooling with the horizontal and vertical adjustments. Television owners lived in dread of picture tube failure. If that happened you might as well just get a new television.

The other wall of the Dairy Bar sported magazine and book racks with much material of dubious quality, the sort of "true men's adventure," genre. As fellow boomer Jay Leno has noted, these publications featured such actual true adventures as Nazi women clad in only bras and panties firing machineguns at the allies. Leno called it a big turning point in the war, a bunch of rag-tag Marines against Hitler's elite D-cup squad.

One could find *True*, *Argosy* and various gazettes, car mags, comic books, movie gossip rags and *Mad* magazine, which many of us read religiously. I once saw among the paperbacks a tome delicately titled *I am a Nympho* with a self-explanatory photograph on the cover. At least the author was up-front about it. My schoolmate Colin Middleton, sometimes tagged "middle leg," procured from those racks a volume called *French Cartoons and Cuties*. Colin, who lived on Dominion, prided himself on being knowledgeable in sexual matters. He was a local version of Ward Stradlater, the "very sexy bastard," in *The Catcher in the Rye*.

Such features made the Dairy Bar the ideal hangout and it provided an informal headquarters for locals, those that Bonny Branch, one of the older girls, called "heroes." The Reaume brothers, Francis or "Fats," as he was known, and the older Leonard, who worked at the White Rose station, were among the regulars. I think Fats might have worked at the White Rose too. Those were the days when stations employed people to pump gasoline, check tires and fluids and wash windows. Tom Ouellette, oldest of 10 children, was capable of cleaning all the windows before the tank had filled. My parents called these places "service stations," and they were. Virtually all of them performed major repairs, which cars of the time needed with considerable frequency.

As I recall, the Reaumes both drove hopped up Fords, Fats a flathead V-8 of that 1949-52 vintage and Leonard a Mercury of the next generation, a sleeker design. John Varney, another regular, drove a black and white 1955 Mercury, with a column stick shift, also known as "three in the tree," the 312 cubic-inch engine, and loud mufflers. He once gave me a ride to Dougall Avenue, but didn't drive very fast, which was what I wanted. Even so I considered the brief ride an adventure. I was a kid but felt part of the in-crowd. We all wanted to be older than we were, and kids would give their age as nine and a half, or "ten going on eleven" and so on. Looking ahead, cars were tied into our concepts of age.

Insurance rates were high for young drivers, for the obvious reason that, as now, such drivers got more tickets and had more accidents. The rates dropped sharply at age 25, so that became a marker for when one was no longer young and reckless, and supposedly entered a life of dull domesticity. So one had to get in all the fun and partying before age 25. It was all wrong of course. One needs insurance to drive, but nobody should look to Allstate and State Farm for the signposts of life. At some point, however, as a comic on BET once noted, one may want to put down that Boone's Farm and pick up some State Farm. My theory is that the true fulcrum of one's life is not any particular age. Rather, it comes when one stops criticizing people older than you and starts criticizing people younger than you. In any case, one can have a lot of fun after 25, and before, while driving and otherwise. I drive, therefore I am, could have been a creed for the Dairy Bar regulars.

Greg Templeton drove a low-slung red 1953 or 54 Mercury convertible and Phil Beaupre a 1956 Ford. Late 1940s Ford coupes with flathead V-8s, and names like "the Gent," or "Lover's Island," painted on the side, and sometimes wolf whistles and aooogah horns, were still around but beginning to give way. The owners of these vehicles could have walked into any movie of the fifties about juvenile delinquents, the *Rebel Without a Cause* types, with little if any costume change.

They wore their hair swept back, and high as a Negro conk, but with the front bunched up and tricking down on the forehead, all very Elvis Presley. Some favored these two wings on the side, swept into a point over the forehead, with the back combed together in what was sometimes called a "duck-ass." The bottom, at the neck, was blocked off in a "squareback" that barbers performed with a straight razor. My mother forbade me to get a squareback in the belief that it was a badge of juvenile delinquency. She was also against carbonated beverages, which included "pop," and did not like comic books. Her own reading included Shakespeare, John Stuart Mill, and Robert Service, also a favorite of my Father, who could rattle off "The Cremation of Sam McGee" with great expression. On a freezing day he would say, "talk of cold, through the parka's fold, it stabbed like a driven nail."

Virtually all of the Dairy Bar regulars smoked, preferring unfiltered cigarettes, Players plain, or Export A. In this crowd, to smoke filtered cigarettes was to be a wimp, to smoke "through a Kotex." Some kept a toothpick in their mouth while they smoked, like Hank at the White Rose station. Rat-tail combs, the best tool for perfecting the duck-ass and its frontal spill, jutted from rear pockets.

The most storied members of this group were the Bertelli brothers, Leonard, Elvino, known as "Vino," and Dickie, all tough guys with a reputation. They had a good-looking sister, Claudia, who did not lack for protection. Guys were afraid to ask her out for obvious reasons. They wanted to live. I have been told that Claudia was Dickie's twin, but that might not be right.

Leonard and Vino were members of the Nomads, probably the city's first motorcycle gang, and Vino's white Triumph Bonneville, with megaphones, which he had sawed off to make them even louder, was often parked in front of the Dairy Bar. For me that bike was a thing of wonder, a truly beautiful machine with clean symmetrical lines. I admired the Bertellis but I was also afraid of them. Dickie once "borrowed" my bicycle and wouldn't give it back. He just left it someplace. I got it back but then I heard that he was "after me." For a while, before actually going to the Dairy Bar, I would peek around the corner at the N&D store to see who was there. There were usually two or three, smoking, sitting on the fender of someone's car, watching girls going by. I can't recall Bud ever chasing them off, and their presence did not deter customers. Maybe Bud preferred to have those guys where he could keep an eye on them.

One of the more entertaining locals was Jerry Piper, not a hot-rod or "hard" type. Jerry would go to mass, and also hang out at the Dairy Bar. He could perform this great Marlon Brando imitation. He even made his face look like Marlon Brando, whom he somewhat resembled in the first place. Jerry was interested in movies and music and you got the feeling he was a deep thinker, even a religious guy in the conventional sense. He didn't mind swearing and wasn't a prude but didn't like it when people said "goddam" and "Jesus Christ." Wiseasses were common in this group, particularly Greg Templeton, who had a quip and insult for everything. But Jerry's was a more genuine humor. He was one of the Dairy Bar regulars, at least one of whom seemed to be there at all times, as though working a shift, waiting for the relief man. The group included some wannabes.

Tunnel Vision

Jim Allsworth, or Aylesworth, was tall, pimply, and looked a bit like Greg Templeton. He wanted badly to be a mainstay of the group, which tolerated him, within limits. According to one story, which I got from Gord Cushman, on a jaunt to Detroit they ejected Allsworth from John Varney's Mercury in the middle of the Detroit-Windsor tunnel, the quickest way to downtown Detroit, but not a place you want to be caught on foot.

It was completed in 1930, long before I showed up, and at the time it was only the third underwater tunnel between two nations. The second was the Michigan Central Railway Tunnel, completed in 1910 also under the Detroit River. I've never been through that one, though it's still in use. They are big on tunnels in this watery part of the world. The first between two nations was the St. Clair Tunnel, from Sarnia, Ontario, to Port Huron, Michigan, site of the famous Port Huron Declaration by Students for a Democratic Society in 1962. At the time, I didn't know anything about it.

The Ambassador Bridge, for its part, was the longest suspension bridge in the world when it opened on November 11, 1929. It no longer held that distinction by the time I first crossed it, but it remains an impressive structure, towering more than 150 feet above the Detroit River. It seems higher when you look down from mid-span, where the view is pretty good. Always a 1,000-foot freighter steaming by in spring and summer, a procession of Edmund Fitzgeralds. That boat, touted as the largest on the Great Lakes, passed our way many times before it sunk in Lake Superior in 1975. Gordon Lightfoot's song mentions a musty old hall in Detroit, the Maritime Sailor's Cathedral, also known as the Mariner's Church, on East Jefferson Ave. It's right by the tunnel entrance and I have passed it many times. Its stained glass window reads:

> Eternal Father strong to save
> Whose arm hath bound the restless wave
> Here us when we cry to thee
> For those in peril on the sea

The Great Lakes may not be a sea, strictly speaking, but you don't want to be caught out there in a storm.

They allowed pedestrians on the Ambassador Bridge, but not the tunnel, though it's well lit and lined with white ceramic tile. The small walkways are barely wide enough for one person. I also heard stories of the Dairy Bar crowd turning someone's car off in the middle of the tunnel, and tossing the keys out the window, a stunt well within the capacity of the people I knew.

Ron Jones, though a bit younger than the Reaumes and Bertellis, seemed to gain more acceptance with the group. A freckly guy with what would be called "sandy" hair that he wore swept back, Ron had this kind of airy, falsetto voice coupled with an occasionally breathless style of speaking that made him an easy target for imitators. He particularly waxed eloquent when holding forth about cars and one of his favorite phrases was "bored and stroked." He knew a lot about cars, as did most of the group, but would summarize modifications to an engine by saying it was "all bored and stroked," giving the impression that he perhaps did not know as much as he let on, a condition true of just about everybody in the neighborhood. Likewise Greg Spindler, brother of Paul, when he found out I took auto shop, asked "can you bore and stroke?" Unfortunately, I couldn't.

"Full moon" hubcaps were popular in those days and the "moon disks" on one local rod bore pictures of scantily clad women which Ron Jones once described as "broad nudes" instead of "nude broads." The image of naked fat women on hubcaps provided some laughs but the freckled Jones was not always congenial. After one softball game at Christ the King, for no apparent reason, he tried to pick a fight with Tommy Ainsor, several years his junior. Tommy, who was on my team, was terrified, but I remember him calling Jones a "rump," not exactly what one would term fighting words. But he stood his ground.

Jones had plenty of company in the surname department. There were in fact, three Bob Joneses in the neighborhood. The younger brother of Kathleen Jones, who lived on the other side of Grand Marais but went to Glenwood school, was not of a scholarly bent, though not in the same class as Johnny Spears or Tommy Durocher. That Bob Jones had a mechanical flair, constructing a crude skateboard out of a toilet seat and metal wheels from roller skates. Polyurethane wheels were not available at the time. Bob's contraption did not prove very agile, though some kids wanted to give it a try.

A more familiar Bob Jones was the youngest of three Jones brothers on McKay, Pete and Tom being the elders. I once got in a fight with Bob for reasons I don't recall, over by the mulberry tree in the vacant lot at the end of our street. It didn't take much to get a fight going. A phrase like "you're ugly and your mother dresses you funny" could do it. People were also baited with phrases like "Ooo, hardness" or "spare me, killer." Clever comebacks included,

"If I want any shit out of you I'll squeeze your head," and "I'll kick your ass so hard you'll look like a hunchback." Also, if someone said "got a match?" the reply could be "yeah, my ass and your face."

In this particular tussle I got in some shots but so did Bob. Ken Morency, older and known as a tough guy, came by on his bike and cheered on my opponent.

"He's already got a fat lip," I remember Morency saying. I did indeed have a fat lip, which made it impossible to hide the fight from my parents. I think I also tore my shirt.

Bob and I quickly patched things up and I used to play pool in their basement, with Danny Timchyshyn, which I heard as "Timtition," a bespectacled, laconic kid who lived next door, and was known simply as "Danny Tim." Pete and Tom were more athletic than Bob, and for a long time Peter worked at Nantais sport shop, a local institution, which we pronounced "Naughtiss." In Windsor most people say "Peery Street" street for Pierre Street, probably the easiest French word to recognize.

Mr. Jones, a wiry bespectacled man who drove a baby blue 1955 Ford, coached little league baseball and I remember him at the Central Park diamond getting into a furious argument with an umpire over what constituted a balk. I think Mr. Jones was correct in that instance.

Yet another Bob Jones lived up near Dougall, tall and blond, almost albino in appearance, with a crafty smile as though perpetually about to deliver a punch line. He spoke softly, as though he feared he might be overheard, and you really had to listen. Bob was a ladies man and his main squeeze was Patti Boyd, a stunning redhead who stood almost as tall as him. He also hung around with the Maxwells, Tom and John, who also lived up there in a tri-level. I knew them pretty well, even though they didn't go to my school. I wasn't in the original class of that school, but I was close.

School so Fair and Square

Glenwood Public School, Area A, Sandwich West Township, stands on Norfolk, across from St. Matthews church, an Anglican congregation. The school opened, I believe, in 1953, maybe 1954. Like just about everything else in the area, Glenwood was built of brick, with a circular driveway out front, and terrazzo floors that have stood the test of time. But for a new building it had some glaring faults.

The stalls in the boys' bathroom, for example, did not have doors. This lapse turned simple evacuation into an involuntary public exhibition, not something most boys are prepared to endure. Hence the stall at the end proved the most popular, even though it was closest to the window and therefore cold. You would freeze your ass, as they say. But during recess and lunch, when there was a lot of traffic, boys declined to use the stalls altogether preferring instead to be excused during class, when they were likely to be alone and avoid humiliation. Based on reports, the girls' bathroom did have doors on the stalls. We complained about this double standard but nothing was done. On the other hand, the bathroom had an electric hand dryer that could be used for a quick warm-up on cold days. You stood so the outlet blasted hot air down your shirt, or into your face.

The absence of doors could have been intended to prevent kids from writing on the walls. The bathroom bards still inscribed verses such as:

Some come here to sit and think
I come here to shit and stink

And so on. Juvenile, yes, but better than the usual fare.

In September of 1955, John Tregaskiss and I were among the kids who made their way to Miss Bell's first-grade class. John, who was born in England, lived on Curry, one street over from McKay, and also home to Pat Sheehan, Ken and Gary Johnson, Glenn Brandt, Gary Stefan, Tommy Durocher, Norm and Laurie Bunny, Anita Totten, Morey Thompson, and Allison and Eddie Lepage. John's older brother, Dave, also went to Glenwood. Dave was one of the few who could contend with Dickie Bertelli, or just about anybody. Clive Tregaskiss, the youngest brother, also went to Glenwood. As they say, Clive could be a discipline problem, but so could we all.

I don't remember much about Miss Bell, but I do recall that the way she sat could be pretty revealing, at least from my viewpoint. I recall a kid, David Lewis, who soon "moved away," as we used to say. Another student, Martin Jerome, had a strange accent but could already write with incredible neatness. He was always upset when Miss Bell would leave the room because the class would quickly degenerate into chaos.

Some of our Catholic friends referred to Glenwood as one of the "Protestant schools," but it was nothing of the kind. We recited the Lord's Prayer in the morning, when we also sang "God Save the Queen," and pledged allegiance to queen and country, but we had none of the special religious instruction they did. On the other hand, I'm not sure that the Catholic schools, called "separate schools," or even the other public schools, had an official song like ours. At Glenwood, they were big on assemblies, and the whole student body would sing:

Glenwood, Glenwood, Glenwood school, school so fair and square.
Kids and teachers strong for you, deny it if you dare!
Red and black the colors are, worn by all who know
Just what school is the best, come and let us show that

This is school is our school and for her we'll strive to
Do our best to fight for might and mane
We will love her, support her, our old alma mater,
Glenwood school of fame.
(refrain)
And when the team goes marching down the field
We know the team, the team will never yield
And though the other team has lots of pep
When they meet our team they'll know they're out of step
And when the team goes down in history,
It's just another Glenwood victory
And all the cheers go out for Glenwood school, Glenwood school
Rah, rah, rah

(cheer)
Kaniny, kanany, kanany, kanoo, with a high-up, sky-up Glenwood
School
(spelling)
G-L-E-N-W-O-O-D, G-L-E-N-W-O-O-D
Yay Glenwood!

Then and now, I have no clue who composed this rousing anthem, probably cribbed from some college fight-song of the 1930s or before. But we would really belt it out, especially the spelling part. So it had a didactic application. The school colors were originally pink and black, later changed to red and black. Some other songs, not heard at assemblies, will be forever associated with Glenwood. One went to a tune from a Disney cartoon.

Hi ho, hi ho, it's off to school we go
We learn some junk and then we flunk,
Hi ho, hi ho.

What we learned wasn't junk at all, of course. At the time it seemed tedious but the education we got at Glenwood was rigorous and as they say "old school." We went through a lot of rote learning, on the multiplication tables and so on, which did us a lot of good, though it didn't always seem that way at the time. Flash cards were standard equipment. The teachers didn't put up with any nonsense and if you didn't know the material you didn't pass. It didn't matter how smart you thought you were, or your parents thought you were, but parents generally went along with the school. If you got in trouble at school you were in trouble at home, big time.

With so many kids, conflict was inevitable. I tussled with Bob Jones and had some schoolyard bouts with Ricky Schroeder, bigger and stronger than me but kind of awkward. John Tregaskiss and I tried to take on the entire class in the second grade. I was skinny as a rake and used to lift weights with Tom Ferri to try and bulk up, with little success. I never had a conflict with advance billing, but one interesting match in school.

We actually had a boxing class at Glenwood and Mr. Hinch, whether intentionally I don't know, paired me with Paul Adams, one of the tougher kids in the school. Proper gloves, a referee, and no possibility of a sucker punch or a kick in the balls all amounted to a level playing field. I found I could hit Paul pretty easily with my jab, and after I landed a few, Hinch even told me to keep punching, so I did, with most of them landing. Hinch didn't let it go on too long. Paul got in some shots of his own but gave me more respect after that. For the most part I tried to stay out of fights, and I admired the tough guys like Dave Tregaskiss, who could take care of the bullies.

Candy of any kind was strictly forbidden in school and gum was right out. The story went around that a teacher got word that a student had blackballs in class. "Who's got blackballs?" she demanded. "Nat King Cole," replied some kid.

Ken Havens once got me in trouble without a television reference. Ken had some artistic talent and would make sketches in class. I think it was in the fifth grade, taught by Mrs. Mann, when Ken was seated behind me. He tapped me on the shoulder and I turned around to see his handiwork.

He had drawn this grinning chef figure, with this huge, billowing chef's hat, and a carrot sticking out of his mouth like a cigar, all captioned "Chef Boy Ardee," a play on the popular food brand. I burst out laughing and got in trouble. Mrs. Mann was all business and once gave me the strap. She really whacked you, across the palm of your hand. But she would get quite embarrassed in "health" courses, when teaching about how the body worked. I remember her using the phrase "trap doors," which we all thought was funny. Somewhere in this discussion the issue of "body odor," came up. If some kid wasn't exactly fragrant, others would say, in a voice as deep as they could manage, "Beeeeee Ooooooo."

A school story I heard from several sources involved a popular game show of the time "The Price is Right," hosted by Bill Cullen. When guests wanted to stand on their answer they would say, "I'll freeze, Bill." A student, possibly Tom Ouellette, pondered the answer to a question when the first bell went off. He didn't know the answer and said "I'll freeze, Bill," upon which the class cracked up. Then when the bell went off again, someone said "bonus! bonus!" another line from the show.

Glenwood's true hot-shot teacher was Miss Zivanovich, first name Bessie. Like Mrs. Mann, she was a no-nonsense type all the way, the kind of teacher that prompts kids to say "boy, is she *strict*." She didn't have much patience with slower kids, like George White and Bobby Kribs, who was destined for trouble. When girls would whisper in class Bessie would say "Who's that Chatty Kathy in the back?" The reference was to a popular doll, advertised on television, that would speak when the owner pulled a string.

Bessie wore dark-rimmed glasses and her sharp facial features made her appear kind of frightening. That could not be said for her friend and colleague, the raven-haired Miss McAllister, an Elizabeth Taylor type with lush eyebrows and long lashes. I never had her as a teacher, alas, but she was often on my mind. I used to wonder what she and Mr. Payne, first name Steve, did in the teachers' room. I know she smoked because I saw her one day when I walked by and the door was open. The principal of Glenwood Public School also smoked.

Norton Mansfield was a tall, short-haired, angular bachelor who walked with long strides and drove a yellow four-door 1960 Ford, a vehicle more suited for a family. Mansfield was, as they say, a controversial figure. Word got around Glenwood that he had a "dead stick," or that he might be "queer." His booming voice could, and did, freeze you in your tracks. But he also had a wit.

Mansfield liked to recite poetry and I remember him reading "Little Bateese," by William Henry Drummond, in the kind of French-accented patois in which it had been written. One line goes "You make me teenk of dem long-legged crane," at which point Mansfield looked at me and interjected "no comments, Billingsley!"

One could fail a grade at Glenwood, but if you were making good progress, they put you ahead. The teachers would have considered ludicrous the notion, common now, that bright, hard-working students should not be advanced on the grounds that it might make others not "feel good about themselves." They advanced John Tregaskiss, one of Glenwood's academic stars, along with Jack Fisher and Michael Bull. As it was brokered to me at the time, I also would have "skipped," but I was six months younger than John.

Michael Bull and I were sufficiently proficient to be named projectionists, allowing us to leave class for the purpose of setting up a film or a film strip. These were mostly boring shorts about such great accomplishments as the hydroelectric dam at Kitimat, British Columbia, though one "health" film had some fleeting nudity. One of the few dramatic efforts, I remember, had the line "Phoebe, goddess of the moon."

One time Miss Zivanovich asked some question and only Jack Fisher and me put up our hands. She kept the rest of the class in for recess. Outside Jack and I compared notes and it turned out that I didn't have the right answer after all. But I did have some advantages.

My mother, Victoria Billingsley, was a substitute teacher. She never taught me in an actual class but she taught just about everyone else in Windsor and she left an impression. When rock and roll was becoming popular, the typical Windsor parent, a product of the big-band era, hated the stuff. Parents would say, "Timmy, turn that damn noisy junk down!" My mother, on the other hand, would take me aside and calmly inform me, "Lloyd, that music is strident and cacophonous." So I had a head start in the vocabulary business.

My brother Phil would see me in the hall at Glenwood and proudly say "that's my brother." That is a wonderful thing but at the time I found it embarrassing. Phil would also try to follow me everywhere, to the point that I had to ask my parents to keep him home. I wanted to hang with kids my age or older, especially John Tregaskiss, whose mother was friends with mine, and who was a terrific public speaker.

One year, in a main assembly, held in the hall, he spoke on "Electricity, Our Servant," with elaborate diagrams showing the generators, stations and substations. As they say, John had done his homework. Another year I thought Kenny Vickers, a short kid with thick glasses, should have won, but Linda Eckert carried the day. I thought she was a teacher's-pet type, and that was true to a point, but she was indeed very smart and articulate. Her family bought one of those new Morris Homes tri-levels, with yellow bricks, on Glenwood

Avenue not far from the school. This was not the same Glenwood Avenue of the 1964 hit by The Pixies Three, but there was surely some resemblance.

Glenwood also featured musical instruction with a certain Miss Holly, a jovial rosy-cheeked woman who would chant "everybody sing, too too tooooo." I didn't much like the singing but I did appreciate the musical theory. She went through the do-re-mi routine and on our first successful harmony the class really lit up.

Miss Holly also taught us the lines and spaces with the standard "every good boy deserves fun," and "face" devices. The musical notation also proved helpful when I started playing clarinet, a gift of my uncle Steve, who lived in Chatham. He also gave me charts for "Don't Get Around Much Any More," by Duke Ellington, and "When the Saints Go Marching In." One year, I joined Bethanne Gillette on alto saxophone, Larry Roy on guitar, and some other Glenwood students in a "Christmas Combo." I don't remember what we played, but it was about the time when I became enchanted with Mo Kaufman's "Swingin' Shepherd Blues," one of the few jazz tunes that got airplay on AM radio. We played in the library, so this concert came before they built the gym and the new wing.

The rule at Glenwood was that you had to walk your bike on the school grounds. The school was big on safety propaganda, and you brought home stuff featuring Elmer the Safety Elephant, whose creed was:

Stop, look and listen, before you cross the street
Use your eyes, use your ears, before you use your feet.

Some kids volunteered for "safety patrol," and stood on the corner, wearing a white belt that went around their waist and diagonally across their chest, holding out their arms out if a car came by. If you didn't obey them they could report you, and sometimes did. Throwing snowballs was also forbidden, too bad because the city's wet snow is ideal for the practice. Kids would say that the snow was "good for packing." One winter it was so cold I tied a scarf around my head. Those earmuffs with the metal band didn't really do the job. While waiting in line to file in, Mr. Fidler, the smallest member of the staff, yelled at me "you with the Russian babushka, stop talking!" The lines had to be straight, or the teachers would yell at you.

The Glenwood curriculum offered no formal sex education but we would sometimes see dogs humping on the school grounds, and also worms would be kind of stuck together. These perhaps illustrate the adage that most of one's education is acquired outside the classroom. This one kid, Don Muzik, described catching his parents in the act, and the details sounded authentic to me. Scott Heydon, not a Glenwood student, also answered many questions when he discovered a trove of nasty porn in his daddy's drawer, and would show it to other kids when his parents weren't home. He called one of the pictures "family reunion" and they had supposedly been taken at a "cat house."

On the playground one heard ditties of a sexual nature that just seemed to come out of nowhere. One went:

Way down in France,
Where the women wear no pants
And the men wear glasses
To see the ladies' asses

In another verse, perhaps by way of retaliation:

The women wear spectacles
To see the men's testicles

The name of one Glenwood teacher, Mr. Bunt, made possible some creative rhymes but you didn't want to get caught at that, or anything else, however innocent. Some kids liked to cup their hand to their armpit then pump their arm to make these great farting noises. Older kids did this too.

They gave the strap at Glenwood, and made you stay "after four," as they used to say. Neither did the teaching staff hesitate to hand out lines, "I will not talk in school," 100 times, that kind of thing. Writer's cramp was a definite threat. In winter, you left your boots in the hall, where other kids would kick them around, resulting in the penalty of writing "I will keep my boots in place" 100 times. Boots were a very necessary item.

When it rained, as it did a lot, puddles spread everywhere. We would often wade through these and you could easily get a "soaker." We learned by direct experience that there are few things in the world worse than wet socks, particularly in cold weather.

Zorro, Dobie, Soupy and Friends

Every classroom had a shallow "cloakroom" at the back, with those accordion doors across the front. You kept lunch boxes in there as well, and it had the smell of bread and peanut butter that seemed to have sunk right into the woodwork. Glenwood had no cafeteria but you could buy milk. The place often smelled like a dairy. On Remembrance Day in November you could buy poppies, and "hot-cross buns," with the money going to veterans.

Mr. Hinch, who used to work at a beer store on Saturdays, once hid in the cloakroom until the class got real loud then burst out swinging a yardstick.

"You've heard of Zorro," he said. "Well this is Hincho."

When the "Zorro" television series was popular, everybody went around making that Z motion. With only three channels, we all watched the same shows, "I Love Lucy," "Leave it to Beaver," "The Life of Riley," with William Bendix, "The Real McCoys" with Walter Brennan and Richard Crenna, the whole lineup that prompted FCC boss Newton Minnow to proclaim television a "vast wasteland." Shows like "Sugarfoot," did hold some appeal, with Will Hutchins packing his rifle and a volume of the law. According to the theme song, he was an "easy loping cattle roping Sugarfoot."

"Perry Mason," with Raymond Burr, as it happens a Canadian, was the first view of a courtroom for many of us, but not the last, as Bobby Kribs was to find out. My father was partial to "Cheyenne," because the star, Clint Walker, was a fellow big man. The theme song asked where Cheyenne would be camping tonight, and wondered where he would finally settle down. As far as I know, he never did. Nick Adams played Johnny Yuma, a rebel who roamed through the west with a sawed-off shotgun.

These were the days of only three major networks and a couple of local channels, but no shortage of programs. Kids of the time would watch virtually anything, even the test pattern, which came on when broadcasting ceased for the day. One of my favorite shows was "The Many Loves of Dobie Gillis," which ran on CBS, channel two in Detroit, from 1959 to 1963. Warren Beatty briefly appeared on it but I don't remember seeing him. I found Maynard G. Krebs, the beatnik played by Bob Denver, to be funny and hip like the show in general. The larger attraction for me was Thalia Menninger, played by gorgeous blond Tuesday Weld. Dobie, played by Dwayne Hickman, had a crush on Thalia. The supposedly brainier Zelda Gilroy, played by Sheila James, had a crush on Dobie, whose "many loves" included Marlo Thomas, Sally Kellerman, Barbara Bain and others, after Tuesday Weld moved on. But she remained my favorite.

I didn't know it at the time, but "Hawkeye and the Last of the Mohicans," starring John Hart and Lon Chaney Jr. as Chingachgook, which sounded like "Chingach-cook," was actually shot in Canada, in Pickering, Ontario. I watched it regularly, along with "The Buccaneers," and "Robin Hood," with Richard Greene.

The "Cannonball" television series was also filmed in Canada, in Bolton, Ontario, and chronicled the truck-driving adventures of Mike Malone and Jerry Austin across the United States and Canada. In one episode a character said, "you make a lousy hundred and fifty bucks a week." At the time it seemed like a lot of money to me.

"Bill Kennedy Showtime," was a local favorite, along with "Shock Theatre." Kennedy, who looked like a kind of middle-age Buddy Holly, would show these old movies and rattle off tales of the stars, as though he had known them. He had apparently been a minor Hollywood actor of some kind. Joan Blondell was one of his favorites. Maybe the two had been on good terms back in the day.

Local hosts for Popeye cartoons included Poopdeck Paul (Paul Allen Schultz), who wore a white sailor's cap, and Captain Jolly (Toby David), who called the kids "shipmates" or "chip mates." The cartoons, though dated even then, remained hugely popular, though they did not make any of us like spinach. We duly came up with a variation on Popeye's theme song.

I'm Popeye the sailor man,
I live in a garbage can
I eat up the worms
And spit out the germs
I'm Popeye the sailor man

I'm Popeye the sailor man
I'm Popeye the sailor man
I stand on the steeple
And pee on the people
I'm Popeye the sailor man

Captain Kangaroo and Soupy Sales were also popular, and Soupy, as Milton Supman was known, first hit it big on WXYZ, Detroit's channel seven, and became the top daytime television personality in the motor cities. His show, "Lunch With Soupy," was on at noon and kids rushed home to watch it. We found the puppets White Fang, Black Tooth, Pookie and Willie the Worm endlessly hilarious. Mr. Sales danced the "Soupy Shuffle" and sported a floppy bow tie, which he would grab at both ends and yell "contact!" when he cut to a cartoon. Soupy would call his viewers "birdbaths," but I don't know how he came up with that term. I loved his weather forecast, with flecks of snow flying out of the radio. The big dramatic moment came when he took a pie in the face, but it wasn't all slapstick. Soupy would offer these gems of wisdom, such as "be true to your teeth and they won't be false to you." He once got in trouble with the Federal Communications Commission for telling kids to go in their parents' wallets, get the green paper with the presidents' pictures on it, and send it to him. Call it taxation without representation.

What had happened on these shows was often a topic of conversation, and imitation. Popeye's muttering, for instance, about some "pesky pachyderm" and such. Many kids would ape "The Three Stooges," with Larry, Moe and Curly, or sometimes Larry, Moe and Shemp, by calling other kids "imbeciles," Moe's favorite word. Some kids could duplicate Curly's whooping gibberish. Or kids would imitate those pokes in the eye that the Stooges performed about every five minutes, sometimes with too much verisimilitude. If a kid did something stupid or clumsy, someone would call him "the one stooges."

Many kids strived to imitate the Tarzan yell, which we heard in old movies with Johnny Weismuller, but only a few succeeded. I doubt whether Johnny actually produced the yell himself but with Jane around in those easy-access outfits, I wouldn't blame him for any spontaneous outburst. And Tarzan always seemed like such a happy guy.

Fun and Games

Before Glenwood had a gymnasium we were pretty much left to our own devices for sports. The full-sized football used in the college and professional games was far too large for our hands. The "pee-wee" football was about seven inches long and a better fit but there was no way to fill it with air and it was usually flat. Even new it was hard to throw a tight spiral with the thing, so we usually did what we could with the full-sized ball. You don't so much throw it as heave it in a shot-put motion but by the time we got to, say, seventh grade we were getting better. Arm strength is the key.

When we played football at Glenwood it was usually Canadian rules, with three downs, though sometimes we played four. Before you started it was settled, American or Canadian rules. Kids followed the Canadian Football League (CFL) and rooted for teams such as the Hamilton Tiger-Cats, then quarterbacked by Bernie Faloney, and the Winnipeg Blue Bombers, who had a fantastic kicker named Chuck Shepherd. He could easily boot a ball 75 yards. The Detroit Lions also had a following but I was a fan of the Baltimore Colts and their great quarterback, Johnny Unitas, and the receiver Raymond Berry. I saw on television the 1958 game in which Berry caught 12 passes and the Colts defeated the New York Giants in overtime. I don't know if it was the "greatest game ever played," as now billed, but it sure held my interest at the time. In other games I also saw a Cleveland Browns running back named Jim Brown, who had also been an all-American lacrosse player at Syracuse. I don't want to argue about it but Jim Brown is the greatest football runner who ever lived.

Tackle football was not allowed at Glenwood, though that would have given the school nurse more to do than sit around. Sometimes we played two-hand touch, which sparked arguments.

"I got you with *two* hands," someone would yell. One-handed touch was easier. Everyone went out for a pass but before you could rush the quarterback you had to count to five saying "rhinoceros," which it supposedly took a second to say, between every number. Sometimes you counted five "steamboats." There were often disputes about whether pass rushers had counted too fast. We served as our own referees. It was the honor system but bad calls were common. More than once some kid decided to take his football and leave, muttering about "cheaters" as he stomped off.

The large Glenwood playground had no formal football field and no yard markings. So you achieved a first down by completing two passes. The strategy in the huddle usually amounted to "go out long," but there were some crossing patterns. The snap count was simply "one-two-three hike." Once however I repeated a poem I had heard on a Popeye cartoon: "Roses are red, violets are blue, gimme the ball, I'm comin' through."

I remember once being guarded closely by Bob Ballance as I went out for a pass. Dave Gourley was the quarterback and I yelled at him "No, Gourley," which he heard as "Now! Gourley." He led me perfectly and I was off for a touchdown. Boundaries were often in dispute, but not on that play. Games would be "continued at recess," or lunch, and you had to remember the score, the down and so on.

Oddly enough, though hockey is Canada's national sport, Glenwood banned hockey sticks on the school grounds. One year they set up a skating rink on the grounds, over by the bike racks, but no hockey took place. In warmer weather, we would play soccer with a tennis ball, a sport we called "foot hockey."

The school did organize intramural games of actual soccer, volleyball and softball. Teachers also got us to play whiffle ball, a stupid, bastardized version of baseball with plastic bats and this goofy plastic ball with holes in it. That ball, about the size of a grapefruit, didn't go far no matter how hard you hit it. This was, I suppose, a lame attempt to equalize the kids. Unfortunately, athletic ability, like intelligence, is not evenly distributed among humankind. Glenwood was evidence of that. On the other hand, whiffle ball enabled play in a confined space, such as the gym.

The school allowed organized games of dodge ball, now under fire in educationist circles as violent and dangerous. In highly technical language, this is bullshit. The ball was soft and about twice the size of a basketball. No kid could throw it very hard, and anybody who could get out of their own way could avoid being hit, which did not hurt.

We also conceived a game called "gob-ball," a kind of dodge-ball in which, if the ball missed you, you spit on it before running away. We used a soccer ball and the one who threw it had to pick it up. We were somehow reported and called down to the principal's office, where Mansfield really chewed us out.

"Spitting and kicking the ball," Mansfield said, with an expression as though he was about to wretch. "Disgusting."

Mr. Hinch also had some harsh words for Rudy Ackerman, a German immigrant, a brilliant student, and easily the best soccer player in school, but who had nevertheless joined in our gob-ball contest. Doubtless he wanted to feel himself one of the guys.

Our early attempts at basketball were pretty pathetic on the outdoor courts, not even paved at the time. In the winter it would rain then the mud would freeze in odd shapes from footprints, making the ball bounce in strange ways. The hoops were hopelessly high, rusty and crooked. Your best shot was a two-handed underhand heave that usually took place in a game of horse. That changed when they put on the addition, with a gymnasium, which was labeled "Gymtorium." We then fielded an official school team, and I discovered that basketball was my game.

The first Glenwood squad featured Barry Campbell, Wayne Shaw, Rick Pfeiffer, Bob Ballance, and myself. Jim Thorne, who was tall, might also have been on the squad, with some others. I remember we lost to Northwood, where Jim Russell, one of the better athletes in the hood, was the star. I scored eight points, which drew praise from Mr. Payne, the bucktoothed teacher with thick glasses, a bad complexion, and usually with a pack of cigarettes clearly visible in his shirt pocket. Mr. Hinch didn't say anything. He thought I was too much of a smartass, and he was right.

Glenwood had a baseball team as well and our ace pitcher was Isaac "Izzy" Novak, who once declined to pitch on Yom Kippur. I think we lost that day.

When we won, the squad would huddle and chant:

One, two, three, four, who are we for?
Glenwood, Glenwood, rah, rah, rah
Five, six, seven, eight, who do we appreciate?
Southwood, Southwood, rah, rah, rah

This chant was also part of local baseball leagues and everybody did it, all part of being a good sport. I have no idea where it came from.

Our major opponent was Central School, whose star player was Ralph Messenger, a big kid and something of a disciplinary problem. He may have failed a grade or two. I remember him smacking a ball right at Mr. Hinch, the Glenwood coach, who was walking away at the time. It narrowly missed his head and that shook him up pretty good. I remember him pointing at Messenger. "You! You there!" I think he took up the case with Central officials.

Team sports were not of course for everyone. Playing was, however, and kids proved good at improvisation. For a while everyone was making these parachutes out of a handkerchief, some string and a fishing sinker or stove bolt for a weight. If folded properly these would unfurl and glide down after you heaved them up as far as you could. I wasn't very good at it, though we had plenty of sinkers at home. You could also buy these kites in a kit, for a quarter or thirty-five cents, and they worked pretty well, though you sometimes had to improvise on the tail.

Spring was marble season, a game virtually all boys played. Many of us made marble games by cutting slots into pieces of wood. If a kid missed the slot, you kept his marble. But if he made it through you had to pay off. The smaller the slot, the bigger the payoff. A whole phalanx of these games would appear along the edge of Glenwood's paved playground, by the bike racks, and it was like a county-fair atmosphere.

"Cats-eye" marbles and "boulders" were sold in plastic bags just about everywhere. Marbles in solid colors were prized but what you really wanted was ball bearings. When playing conventional games, in which you got the other guy's marble by hitting it, these would destroy the opposition. They were your "shooter." Ball bearings weren't sold in the usual places so you needed connections of some kind to get them.

Some of the marbles were so pretty we just collected them, setting them apart from the rest, which we kept in cloth bags. Another collectible was a piece of limestone with a quartz cluster in it. We called these a "jeel," and they could be found sorting through the rocks they put on streets before paving. It took quite a while to find them. I remember Linda Eckert, the smart girl a year older than me, who had won the public speaking contest, asking what I was looking for on her street. She wondered if I had perhaps lost something. Or maybe she just wondered what I was doing near her place.

Bolo bats were the rage for a time, rather easy to master but the elastic often broke. These toys later made a film appearance in *Blazing Saddles*, in which Governor William LePetomane (Mel Brooks) wants to "hand these out to the boys in lieu of pay."

The hula hoop became the craze du jour, and may have contributed to back trouble for many kids and some adults. Yo-yos were in pretty much all the time and I want to say the best brand was "Ace." The good ones had these little rhinestones that sparkled when the thing spun. The standard tricks included: walk the dog, around the world, rock-a-bye baby, and making the yo-yo "sleep," that is, spin in one place. I spent a lot of time untangling my yo-yo, and if the string came off, it was hard to get it right again, though my dad could tie a good slip knot.

The Glenwood girls jumped rope and had this other game, "yogi," in which they stretched out this elastic between two girls and another swung her leg over it back and forth as the others chanted some rhyme. The guys thought it was pretty stupid and many years later one of the girls confirmed that it was.

More formally, Glenwood held various "fun fairs" with a fish pond and various games. These good-clean-fun events, sanctioned by the school, were looked down on somewhat. But "hard" types, with their collars turned up, would still show up because, as Chuck Berry said, they had no particular place to go. That was a common condition at the time.

Some friendships started at Glenwood have lasted a lifetime. But in the hood at that time, one's friends also came from outside the classroom.

Mechanical Advantage

One of my first friends was Jimmy Dugal, who lived on the corner of Curry and Norfolk, right across from Glenn Brandt, and to one side, across Norfolk, Randy Essery. I walked right by there on my way to Glenwood. Jimmy went to Christ the King school, also known as Notre Dame, with Mark Lantz and many others, but we hung out all the same. Jim's father was known for romping with his kids in bed in the morning, holding them under the covers and farting, something he called the "Dutch oven" treatment. When not so occupied, Mr. Dugal would go for long walks in the country to keep himself in shape. He was a serious man and much greater than the sum of his farts.

Jim's older brother Tom was one of the Dairy Bar regulars, though in some ways more sophisticated. I remember him telling me about someone who moved to London, "because he could swing there." I once impressed Tom by reciting a verse of "Tell It Like It Is," by Aaron Neville, when Tom asked me if I knew the words.

Tom once worked at Kelsey Wheel company, one of the many "feeder" industries for Chrysler and Ford. The joke went around about "Tom Dugal and the Kelsey Wheels," based on Mitch Ryder and the Detroit Wheels, a popular band. But Tom didn't think it was very funny.

Tom and Jimmy shared a room in the basement, and for a time even the same bed, an arrangement by no means uncommon, and one that that my brother Phil and I practiced for a time after Ralph was born in 1956, the only member of our family born in Windsor. I recall Tom yelling at Jimmy because he had been eating crackers and some crumbs dropped in the bed on Tom's side.

Jimmy had at least three sisters, all but one older. He stuttered, pretty badly at times, which led some to believe that that Jimmy wasn't very smart, which wasn't true. Jimmy had plenty of smarts, just not the kind then being cultivated in schools by politicians looking for our generation to be the Leaders of Tomorrow. This type, though scoring well on school exams, often lacked the ability to change a tire. As for Jimmy, he was right off the mechanical charts.

He could take anything apart and put it back together again, and probably do it blindfolded. And he also saw what wasn't there. I once went around the corner at the Metropolitan store and saw Jimmy gliding along about four feet above the rows of parked cars. He had taken apart his bicycle and flipped the frame, so the pedals were at the top, not the bottom. He then reversed the front fork and rigged special tubing for the handlebars and seat, a set-up that lofted his head to the altitude of a basketball rim, higher than Wilt Chamberlain. Jimmy didn't do it to get attention but of course he did. The dismount was a problem, so once he got going he just kept riding. He had to lean against the side of a building to get off.

This creation alone secured his reputation and inspired various attempts at imitation, one by the Bob Jones the guy who improvised the skateboard out of a toilet seat. But he couldn't match Jim's ingenuity.

Jimmy later went though a series of cars, proving himself adept at bodywork and painting. But their house on Curry had no garage and when the parts piled up in the driveway, Mr. Dugal would scream at him. He evidently thought, like all our parents, that the purpose of working on a car was to build something you could drive for years. Jimmy was one of those who whipped up a masterpiece then got rid of it and started again on some 1954 Pontiac, with fenders painted in gray primer. The process, not the product, was the thing.

In Windsor the snow would melt, freeze, then get covered with snow again. This put down a layer of ice and packed snow ideal for hitching rides on the bumpers of automobiles, a practice more dangerous than crossing the pipe over the Grand Marais Ditch. But in our world fun usually trumped danger, and skiing along behind a car was fun indeed, though you could catch a face full of exhaust. When a bunch of us would wander around on winter nights, Jim would approach a car at an intersection and flash all sorts of spastic arm movements. This surely left many drivers bewildered.

When a car passed, we would sometimes thump on their fender, then one of us would fall down and writhe around in the snow as though he had been hit. If they stopped to see what had happened, our wounded colleague would stay down just long enough to strike fear before getting to his feet and bolting with the rest of the gang.

Jim held strong opinions about automobile style, and derided those little dingly balls that people would drape around their interior as "monkey's nuts." Other trends included bubble skirts, lake pipes, and dual spotlights at the lower corners of the windshield. People put names on cars and it was popular to trick out vehicles with custom tail-lights, rolled pans, and to "nose and deck" the car, removing chrome and emblems on the hood and trunk. Some even removed the door handles and I still don't know how they got in and out. The high roofs of the time were "channeled" for a lower profile, and cars generally rode low. The motorboat look, high in front, low in rear, was also popular. Continental kits were still acceptable, particularly on low-slung four-doors like the late-1940s, early-1950s Mercury, with the "suicide doors." Interiors were laid out for comfort, with a variety of seat covers, and sometimes goofy stuff like dice hanging from the rear-view mirror. These trends, part of the "custom car" cult, put style over speed, but eventually gave way to the muscle-car craze.

I remember asking Wayne Offen, who lived further down on McKay, near Curry Park, how he would alter a car. He said he would "customize it down," which I took to mean that he would lower it. Wayne's father made particular use of one popular automobile accessory of the day, those plastic knobs you screwed on the steering wheel, which helped compensate for the lack of power steering, an option thought by some to be extravagant or unnecessary. It was all "more shit to go wrong," as some parents would say.

Mr. Offen had one arm, but he got around in a blue Ford station wagon, a 1955 or 1956, with help from one of those knobs. Some knobs bore pictures of women, what Ron Jones might call "broad nudes" but more likely slender semi-nudes. I remember Morey Thompson arguing that knobs with such pictures had been banned because they distracted drivers and caused accidents. Where Morey got this information I don't know. Many of us were in the habit of making wild or authoritative statements without sensing any need to cite a source. Some would claim, for example, that you could drive without insurance under a government plan called "unsatisfied judgment," which sounds like a television movie. It wasn't true.

I don't know what sort of picture, if any, adorned the knob on Mr. Offen's Ford, but I do know he could sure wheel that thing. I remember my dad saying that Mr. Offen's one arm was likely strong as two of anybody else's. He was reportedly a big-time drinker and one wall of their basement bore a poem about Canadian drinking habits, how they "drink the whole damn business." Bob Offen, Wayne's older brother, was good at telling jokes. He once told me I would laugh at anything, which wasn't true. I called him "Boffen," and he was touchy when anybody pointed out that his initials were BO.

Glenn Brandt, who lived right across from Dugal, was a couple of years older and hung out more with the Tregaskiss brothers and the Curry Avenue crowd. But we were friends. I remember Glenn telling me, as we were about to begin a baseball game at recess, that this was the "Grade five diamond," and that we would have to move. He was pals with Gordy Moore, who lived on McKay, on my paper route, and whose family owned a Keeshond dog.

Tregaskiss, Brandt, Offen, Lantz, Hannan, Dugal, Roy. These were all my neighbors and schoolmates, along with scores of others. I knew kids from school, from sports, from church, and just from hanging out. That was true of everybody in the hood. There were people just beyond the borders of our neighborhood, however, who were also "outside" in a different sense.

A family I will call Rollins, who lived across Huron Line, had a different concept of hygiene than most of us and coherent speech was not their strong suit. I never learned what the parents did, if anything. They lived in a dumpy house on a dirt road, where most of the lots were vacant and choked with weeds.

The eldest son, whom I will call Josh, was a wannabe badass who would try and impress Greg Templeton, Varney and the senior Dairy Bar crowd by telling them he knew Johnny Banks, a local stock-car driver of some reputation who also ran an auto shop, Banks Alignment. Templeton used to mock Rollins mercilessly, and it was hard to see how he didn't deserve it. Once, in the parking lot of the N&D, Gregg and his buddies were sitting in his convertible smoking and listening to the radio, when Josh came up and sprung the Banks query.

"Banks? Yean, I know him," Templeton said. "Ernie Banks," a reference to the shortstop of the Chicago Cubs, their first black player. Templeton used a different adjective, and the other guys in the car thought this was very funny.

Josh postured as a tough guy but wouldn't pick on anybody his own size. A solid six-footer, he didn't come across as a guy who could handle himself "in a beef," as we used to say. His complexion got him tagged "pizza face," and "dartboard." Josh talked and looked like the skinny, black-jacketed tough who later appeared on the television show "Shanana." He had aspirations to be a musician but there wasn't a musical bone in his body. He admired one of my friends and classmates, Larry Roy, a fine guitar player, but pronounced his name "Larry Row."

During the mid-1960s, Josh wanted to start a band called the Dartels, but there already was one, with "Hot Pastrami" on the charts in 1962. He also aspired to the car scene and eventually procured a blue 1956 Ford Crown Victoria, the one with that gaudy chrome strip across the roof, with the 312 cubic inch V-8, stick shift, dual exhaust, whitewall tires and those smaller rear fender shirts. It could have used a paint job but wasn't in bad shape. But by then that model had ceased to be a local favorite, giving way to the Mustang, Camaro, Chevelle and Chevy II. Josh favored black leather jackets and I have heard stories of him on a motorcycle, a scary thought. But I never saw him riding one.

By one account, I think from Lyle Goulet, Josh knocked a hole in a bedroom wall so he could watch his sisters undress. Barry, a younger brother, reportedly was in the habit of telling his own father to "fuck off." They supposedly had a kid brother named Tobias, although this may have been something invented by Lyle Goulet.

Not many families shared this profile or lived in such conditions. On the other hand, few flaunted their wealth. To be sure, upscale custom homes could be found nearby, in a neighborhood just across Dougall, but none of my friends lived there.

Hardness

E ven in the motor cities you couldn't drive until the age of 16. In our pre-driving days, getting to downtown Windsor was not a problem on the SW&A bus system, the Sandwich, Windsor and Amherstburg line. It was best not to ride one's bike downtown. It was dangerous and they got stolen. If you were going to Detroit, which we did without a second thought, the bus was the way to go. It dropped you off right at the tunnel, which we used regularly. The drivers gave you change from those metal dispensers they wore on their belts, and they put the coins on a shallow metal dish, not in your hand, so they could keep their eyes on the road. Call it an early version of multi-tasking.

We slipped over to Detroit for shopping, not for movies, which were the same Hollywood fare in both cities. Windsor boasted the Palace, Capitol, Tivoli and Vanity theatres. Kids would line up around the block for hokum like *Journey to the Center of the Earth*, with that great star Pat Boone, horror schlock like *The House on Haunted Hill*, and epics like *Ben Hur*, with Charlton Heston. Films such as *Butterfield 8* were rated "adult entertainment." The balcony at the Palace was always crowded, and some kids would make squawking noises by blowing into empty candy boxes. The ushers would toss you for that, and for throwing popcorn on those below.

I would also take the bus to the YMCA on Pelissier, where the rule was that everyone had to swim nude, a rule that did not apply to the girls, though I was never able to verify it empirically. The reason for the nude regime was never explained, and to this day I don't know how they got away with it. I do know I hated it and eventually switched to Kennedy Collegiate, where you could wear a bathing suit. The showers also took forever to warm up.

Near the YMCA was a narrow phone-booth of a place called the Espresso Toro Coffee House, where you would see people in berets and sweatshirts, beating on bongos. It was Windsor's part of the beatnik craze, which Larry Roy and I got into, big time.

On the way downtown you also passed the Elmwood Hotel, a place I never entered but which hosted such big-time acts as Sammy Davis, Jimmy Durante, the Supremes, Louis Armstrong, Nipsy Russell, Milton Berle, and, a bit later, Glenn Campbell. The Top Hat, right downtown, also drew big names. The Killarney Club, on Wyandotte, had two floor shows a night.

On a bus ride home, when I was about 10, I first saw Ken Durocher, or Desrosiers, then an aspiring tough guy, who was taunting another passenger for no apparent reason.

"Who do you think you are, king shit?" I remember Ken saying. It was the first time I had heard this phrase, which I thought was really funny, rather than menacing. I later heard it expanded to "Who do you think you are? King shit on Turd Island?" But I was also afraid of Ken Durocher that day.

He told the passenger, a younger, smaller kid who had done nothing to provoke him and was obviously terrified, to meet him later that day at the Blue Bell Motel on Huron Line, where they would have it out. Ken, not yet known as "Skinny," lived over that way. I don't know what happened but my guess is that neither party showed up. Other times both parties definitely did. While our hood wasn't as rowdy as the Drouillard Road area, you'd have to say it was a pretty rough neighborhood. Pretty much everybody got challenged at one time or another. You would hear it said of someone that "he couldn't fight his way out of a wet paper bag with both ends open."

Nobody wanted that to be said of them. I remember Mark Lantz saying of this one skinny kid that "he probably sprained his wrist wiping his ass" and "dove into bed too hard and cracked three ribs."

The tough guys we described as "hard," or a "hard rock," and certain styles and manners designated hardness, a status to which many aspired. Even friends would sometimes greet each other with a short punch to the shoulder, which I can testify really hurt. There were also "slap fights," a kind of half-way house between shadow boxing and a real fight sometimes indulged between two friends to find out who was faster with his hands, and to test endurance. I believe Bob Olteen, aka Poojie, and Dave Drayton, once matched slaps. But there was plenty of outright combat.

A fellow I will call Hank Murdock had failed several grades at Central School and was nearly able to drive to class in the eighth grade. He was a classic bully with no shame, a real delinquent, as they used to say, and known around the neighborhood as kind of a predator. They used to flood those tennis courts at Central Park for skating. I was coming across the park, returning from Lyle's place, or maybe Woolco, when I saw Murdock at the edge of the courts, under the lights, his back to me. There were a dozen or so people skating.

I couldn't see what Murdock was doing but he must have been exposing himself because I heard him say, "Have you ever seen an adorable cock like mine?"

The skaters, including some adults, quickly disbanded and I took the long way around. Murdock was pretty good at terrifying younger kids like me, but he couldn't avoid a showdown with those, as they say, his own size. Dave Tregaskiss would have easily "hung a job on him," a phrase we used for a decisive victory. Hank knew it and avoided Dave. But Murdock apparently shot his mouth off and said he could beat up Bob Adams, an older guy I didn't know very well. Word got around and the two finally met at Curry Park, over by the baseball diamond.

I was there that day, and the place was packed. Kids were walking around saying things like "in this corner, the heavyweight champ. . . " and "get your peanuts, popcorn" etc. Murdock got there first and was doing his tough guy act, pretty much all by himself. He didn't have a lot of friends or supporters for obvious reasons. Adams took a while to show up but when he did, he didn't indulge in any posturing.

The two squared up and Adams got right to it, fists and feet flying. This was the real stuff, no fake Hollywood haymakers and sound effects, just as when Dickie Bertelli took down the intruder outside the Dairy Bar. The rest of us formed a rough ring around the fighters, giving them plenty of room. Adams did not have the hardness look, but he quickly got the best of it, to the undisguised delight of the spectators, many of whom were afraid of Murdock and had been bullied by him. It was over fast and no cops showed up or anything like that. People were talking about it for quite a while.

Such battles had no rules other than beat the living shit out of the other guy before he beat the shit out of you. In mixed company people would sometimes say "beat the snot out of you."

Nobody brandished knives, guns or anything like that, and scratching and biting were frowned on, but otherwise you used all your natural assets. It was important to be fast with your feet, to be able to "shoot the boots," and you would see people practicing, flicking their feet out, usually about groin level but often way up high. Gordie Moore, who lived in the next block of McKay, once came up to me in Curry Park and, a propos of nothing, kicked me square in the nuts. Anyone who has endured such an attack will understand that pain doesn't get any worse, and that an accurate boot to the groin, especially with the pointed shoes of the time, renders you completely helpless. There was much debate about who had the "fastest boots in Windsor."

One candidate was Murray Loomis, a teenager with dark-rimmed glasses and a kind of Roy Orbison look that might have been intentional. I knew him from this pool where he served as a lifeguard and I remember him raving about Roy Orbison records like "Crying" and "Only the Lonely," and about the cover on one of Orbison's albums, where the singer is all dressed in black and getting out of a limo. Murray was himself a pretty suave guy by local standards and had a thing with Karen Kirkwood, a pretty brunette with light freckles who went to Southwood school. In Curry Park, Karen once smacked a kid who grabbed one of her boobs and twisted it.

I never saw Murray Loomis fight anybody so I don't know if his reputation was deserved. I do know he thought he was pretty tough. I asked him what he thought of the Bertelli brothers and he pretty much wrote off the whole bunch, especially Elvino.

"Vino got his reputation beating up people like you," Loomis told me, with undisguised contempt.

I have no way of proving it, but my sense is that any of the Bertellis, even Vino, who did have kind of a big gut and moved slowly, would have made short work of Murray Loomis.

Mike Marcenko, a narrow-eyed rather short guy with sandy hair that never seemed to move, was a sometime member of the Dairy Bar crowd and also known as having fast boots, supposedly the fastest in town by some accounts. Mike wasn't much of a talker. I never saw him in action, but you got the feeling that he could handle himself. His reputation was unquestioned.

Bob Cushman, though not of great stature, also had fast feet. But he was in the Nomads so he was surrounded by tough guys who stuck up for each other. For a while Bob drove a blue 1957 Mercury, one of the more radically styled cars of the time, in addition to his Triumph motorcycle. I was friends with Gord Cushman, his younger brother, a great sprinter despite an early case of rheumatic fever that left him with some kind of heart trouble. You could see this big vein pulsing in his neck. When Gord and I rode in the Mercury it was quite an event. It was loud but not as loud as Bob's modified Triumph 650. When Bob roared by Glenwood School it rattled the windows and literally stopped class. I think Mr. Mansfield, the principal, might have called the cops at one point. He didn't like any competition in the volume department.

As noted, Bob was a member of the Nomads. I too was briefly in a bicycle gang called the Disciples, founded by Mark Lantz, Jimmy Dugal and myself. Though an obvious imitation of the Nomads, whom we all revered, it was actually more of a club. This was long after the stage when you did things like clothespin playing cards so they flapped in your spokes – though we did do that. In the Disciples we tricked out our bikes with those high-rise handlebars and custom seats. We also removed the fenders and chain guard, even though this mean that water splashed up on your back, and you often got your pants caught in the chain. Few kids wore shorts in those days. If possible, you gave the frame a "candy apple" paint job, a task for which I was ill suited. The paint kept orange peeling on me. Jim Dugal, now there was someone who could paint, with a "spray bomb," as we called an aerosol can, or anything else. He knew how to sand and lay down the proper primer. I was too impatient for all that.

Our stripped-down bikes stood in distinction to the junked-up rigs with mudflaps, generators and lights, carriers, saddlebags, and all sorts of reflectors. It was acceptable in the Disciples, however, to have a pair of clearance lights, purchased from Canadian Tire, on your real axle. Our bikes were the motorless equivalent of the sleek Triumphs, BSAs and Nortons favored by the Nomads. The other bikes were the equivalent of full-dressed Harley Davidsons, the only kind we ever saw, with saddlebags, windshields, multiple headlights, and even a continental kit in one case. The first Harley "chopper" we saw was in the movies, well into the 1960s. Marlon Brando rode a Triumph in *The Wild One*. Lee Marvin, who bore considerable resemblance to my father, rode a Harley-Davidson.

We even had a tenth-mile bicycle drag strip on one of the newly paved streets near Glenwood. Someone, I think Bob Cushman, measured it for us with his car, using the odometer's tenth-mile gradations. We also paced it off after some calculations. We left tire marks by the starting line, as though we all did burnouts.

Gord Cushman beat me in one of these tenth-mile races, but that was because I tried to squeal my tires at the start. I was pretty good at that, but not at the wheelstands and power slides that were a mark of prowess within the group. These were all one-speed bikes, with coaster brakes. Few kids owned three-speeds, usually Raleighs with leather seats as hard as concrete, and that little shifter you flipped with your thumb. The Sturmey-Archer gears were all inside the rear hub and the shifting cable led to a little chain that went in there. Once these things broke it was hard to fix them, even though the mechanism is pretty simple. Joe's Bicycle shop, on Erie St., was the place. His yellow logo could be found on the frame of many a bike in Windsor. We had heard of 10-speeds but I don't think anybody owned one. I believe Gord Cushman defeated a three-speed in a tenth-mile drag. Shifting took valuable time.

I remember Tom Dugal having a laugh over our gang, as an obvious imitation of the Nomads. They had a clubhouse, over by Howard Avenue, near Merrifield's body shop, whose official car was a burgundy 1959 Chevy El Camino with lake pipes and bubble skirts. The Nomads, meanwhile, did not have Windsor all to themselves.

The Queensmen, a similar group, also plied the streets on their Triumph, BSA, and Norton motorcycles. The Erie Ramblers, out of Chatham, used to hang around Rondeau Park, though I never saw them in Windsor. I remember one Nomad, a tall rather gaunt guy with a straggly beard, with a vague resemblance to actor Clint Walker. Another member had rigged his Triumph with a rigid frame and these two narrow aluminum tanks that looked more like tubes. Most of the bikes had custom paint jobs, with pinstriping on the tank and matching colors on the tach and speedometer housings. And of course the engines had been hopped up. When the Nomads came roaring down the street, it was quite an event. When you heard them talking amongst themselves, the name of Bert Appleyard often came up. He ran some Triumph shop over on Howard and had the reputation of being a cantankerous man.

Windsor was also home to car clubs such as the Streetcleaners, Challengers and the El Draggos, who used to meet at the home of the Matthesons, on McKay, right next to our house. I admired one of the 1932 Ford coupes. Each car had this little metal plaque, with the club name, mounted by the back window.

The Disciples found some competition in the Nomadic Knights. I remember telling Jim Dugal and Jim Janisse, who lived in a big brick place on Grand Marais, that the Nomads would not look kindly on a name like that. We never had rumbles, but on one occasion someone sawed off a member's riser bars. The victim might have been Mark Lantz, and if we knew who did it, we would have hung a job on him. Or maybe not.

Though not in gangs, most kids had a close circle of friends. Families did things together, more of a rule than an exception.

Better Living Through Chemistry

When my parents wanted to take us out on a Sunday, they usually went to the Knotty Pine restaurant on Dougall. I once tried to get a job there as a busboy but it didn't happen and I was pretty disappointed. At the time I wanted to break free from my paper route. Bus-boy work was inside, and no heavy lifting. Whatever the job, we all enjoyed ample time for trivial pursuits.

We used to play this game of switching the letters of each other's first and last names. John Hartloff became Hohn Jartloff, Mark Lantz, Lark Mantz, and so on. I remember Bob Ballance pointing out that he was immune for obvious reasons, but John Hartloff said no, that you simply moved on to the second letter, making him Bab Bollance. I was straight up Boyd Lillingsley.

Actually, my rather long last name got me tagged "Bills," for short. This happened around the time of a popular song, "Don't Mess with Bill," that now became "Don't Mess with Bills." Variations included "Wills" and "Swills." I'm not sure who came up with Swills – it wasn't me – but it might have been Jim Dugal, Mark Lantz, Lyle Goulet, or John Tregaskiss. In any case, it stuck. It wasn't what I would have chosen, but I accepted it. By contrast, other names were chosen by the bearer.

Morrie Thompson, who lived on Curry, near John Tregaskiss, insisted on being called "Scott" or "Scottie," a strange demand I mostly ignored. Morrie was a buck-toothed kid with a kind of nasal tone of voice and often mysterious, kind of sinister manner. You got the feeling that he was always plotting something. And he gave the impression of vast experience.

We would be prowling through Rankin Bush, which was pretty dense, and he would send me on these scouting missions, to find "forts" that other kids had put up. One day I remember him telling me, as though he were Davy Crockett himself, that "a good scout doesn't come back until he's found out what he's supposed to find out." In a way, Morrie was right because it paid to do some scouting.

You never knew who or what you would find in the woods. There were various "lovers' lanes," where people would be parked in a two-tone 1955 Chevy, watching the submarine races. Some kids tried to catch a peek at what was going on, but I steered clear of these situations.

I had heard the stories of "Slingshot Louie," who lurked in Bozo Bush, north of Third Concession. If this guy caught you, rumor had it, he and his gang would strip you naked, hold you down, and blackball you, that is, spray-paint your balls black, and nobody wanted that kind of cruel and unusual punishment. I foolishly went out to Bozo Bush by myself one day and did encounter a group of kids with slingshots. One of them picked off this frog in an abandoned well. The leader had close-cropped blond hair and a squint, but he didn't give his name. He wasn't exactly friendly, but took no action against me. I didn't hang around long in any case. I had resolved, at least, that Slingshot Louie did not have existential problems.

Lyle Goulet simply announced one day that he was to be called "Rocky," a mandate with which not everybody complied, though I did hear him called "Rock." Lyle wasn't any kind of a physical specimen but tended to single out kids who looked vulnerable. At a Glenwood fair he cornered Stuart Galloway, a scrawny, scholarly kid with wispy hair who wore wire-rimmed glasses.

"Hey kid," Lyle said. "You want a gob right in the eye?"

"That's debatable," Stuart responded, as though it had been a question from his science teacher. This disarmed Lyle, who still thought Galloway a hopeless case.

Lyle once treated his hair with peroxide and it came out orange as a traffic cone, not something a hard guy would do. But Lyle did get called a lot of things for a lot of reasons.

He lived over on Morris drive, the last house before Cabana, with his father and brothers Roger and Wayne, who was almost totally deaf. They used gestures and grunts when talking to Wayne. I don't recall what had happened to Mrs. Goulet but Mr. Goulet I remember well. He was bald, with thick glasses that made his eyes look like boiled eggs. He yelled at his kids, particularly Lyle, who could usually be found in the basement working with his chemistry set, the most extensive I had ever seen. I remember being down there one day. The radio was playing "The Bounce," by the Olympics. But the chemistry set was not the ideal equipment for someone of Lyle's inclinations. He was the kind of kid who gets tagged a shit disturber or a wiseass, all of which he deserved and more. He usually wore the kind of expression that could prompt an adult to say "and wipe that look off your face."

The Metropolitan store in Yorktown Square boasted an extensive candy counter and I remember Lyle ordering a bag of ju-jubes by saying "give me some of that noise there." While the guy was scooping the stuff out, Lyle would scowl and tell him, "too many black ones." But kids didn't always enter stores to buy.

Shoplifting, also known as "five-finger discount" and "scoffing," was rather common in the hood, a kind of rite of passage. It was mostly petty stuff, candy, small toys, sometimes tools. But it was after all stealing, illegal, a crime. One particularly skillful shoplifter wore special oversized "scoffing pants," as he called them, and even a "scoffing coat." I witnessed one kid shoving a popsicle down his pants at the Dairy Bar, lamely explaining when caught that had bought it "at the other store."

Johnny Longmore was working at the Metropolitan store and took me aside one day and told me that a neighbor of mine had better watch his step if he knew what was good for him. There was a story going around that one kid made off with an entire road-race set from Woolco, and that another got caught stealing a slinky toy at the same place.

Hit Parade

The grand opening of the Woolco department store on Dougall was truly a major event. No longer did residents of our hood have to drive to the Sentry department store, or downtown. People mobbed the place and Lyle Goulet took full advantage. Before the store was officially open, he walked past the cord barrier, only to be turned out by a guard. That day Lyle wore this hat with a long blue feather. He would stand in front of people and move his head from side to side, so the feather would whip across their faces. He really got kicks from pissing people off and the rest of us found this great entertainment.

Woolco was the ideal hangout, with a cafeteria at the back where you could buy burgers and fries. The sporting goods department sold these thin, butterfly knifes that you could pretty much flick open, and are probably illegal now. The jewelry department sold "friendship rings" that some guys bought for girls they were "going around" with. Kids also sought out the automatic photo booth.

You got in, drew curtains, put some change in a slot and it snapped three pictures. After about a minute these came rolling out of an outside slot, accompanied by the stench of chemicals. A lot of clowning went on in that booth. Some wanted to take racy photos but hesitated because the company retained the negatives and kids were afraid they would somehow track them down. Still, there was a rumor that some guy had taken a picture of his privates, and that a local girl had bared her breasts for the camera.

The pinball machines in Woolco's small arcade were not as good as the one at Ashton's Motel, in my opinion. Most of the time we hung around the record department, where a black felt board proclaimed the current top-ten hits. The white letters were easy to rearrange, which we did.

"Venus in Blue Jeans," for example, by Frankie Avalon, became "Penis in Blue Jeans," and "Rambling Rose," by Nat King Cole, became "Rambling Nose." Jan and Dean's "Surf City," became "Sift City," which may have got by most people. Among our group, a common mispronunciation for the disease syphilis was "siftless" or "siffless." People would say that a certain easily accessed girl was "sifty." One couldn't go out with her because "No way I want to get sift." So "Sift City" seemed a natural. In the same vein, I also heard someone say that a certain girl had "crotch crickets." I remember the older guys talking about getting crabs from certain girls, and how this required a special "blue ointment" to cure. You couldn't be too careful. There was also a legend that in sex a girl could "clamp up on you," so you couldn't break free. You were trapped.

It was a kick to watch people come up and read the board with our alterations as you leafed through the LPs. Another possibility, though one I never saw pulled off, was "Running Bear," which could have been Running Bare. When the Johnny Preston song was popular, people would come up and ask if you liked "running bare," then laugh if you said yes. Call it an early attempt at the double entendre. When we would sing along with this tune we changed the lyrics to "now they'll always be together, in the happy grunting hound." This kind of alteration was common.

Recall for example "If You Want to be Happy for the Rest of Your Life," by Jimmy Soul, one of the many one-hit wonders. The song urges you to marry an ugly woman because, unlike a pretty woman, she will give you "peace of mind." That phrase got changed to a piece of something else that didn't exactly rhyme.

The album covers by the Ventures, a popular guitar group that scored a hit with "Walk Don't Run," always featured scantily clad women. So did those by Chuck Berry. "Sweet Little Rock and Roller" showcased this blond with a cigarette in her mouth and, as far as I could tell, wearing only a motorcycle jacket.

"The Lion Sleeps Tonight," by the Tokens, had this chanting chorus of "a weem-a-weh, a weem-a-weh, a-weem-a-weh." Paul Adams told me one of his friends thought they were singing, "my wiener's wet, my wiener's wet." The flip side of the record was a tune called "Tina" in the same faux-African style. It wasn't until years later I learned that the Tokens were all white guys from Brooklyn. The flip side of the "Monster Mash," by Bobby "Boris" Pickett, was another attempt at the macabre. Many years later the Toys turned Bobby's opus into the "monster hash" complete with a "personal stash."

The song about Alvin's harmonica, speeded up to make it sound like chipmunks, was a natural sing-along. We would also sing along to tunes with ludicrous lyrics, such as these from Johnny Horton's "Sink The Bismarck." The ship's guns were "big as steers," and the shells "as big as trees."

The 45 rpm records, the compact discs of the time, were cheap and we loaded up on them. If your record player had the proper gear you could stack them up, just as you could with 78s or 33s. That was helpful because few songs lasted even three minutes. Or you could play them one at a time with this little plastic thing that went in the hole. If you didn't have that you had to carefully place the record, and if you got it off center the singers sound drunk.

In front of Woolco stood a yellow St. Vincent de Paul bin for used clothing donations. When people were filing into the store, Rick Michalski used to run past them, crash into this thing, then crumple into a pile. Another time he managed to get inside the bin and terrify passers by like some kind of ghost. Rick also told the security guard that he would never become a policeman and that he should deal with it.

Woolco was not the limit for Lyle Goulet's capers. He once tossed some potassium permanganate into Central Pool, turning the water purple. The pool always had a big exhibition night, at the end of the summer, when the lifeguards, Barb Bouffort in particular, performed their special dives. I remember Danny Metcalf, a lifeguard, trying to pull off a swan dive with a full twist, with mixed success. He entered the water sideways with a huge splash. That night Lyle climbed on the roof of the pool building, where the alert announcer spotted him. He somehow dropped down and scurried away. The next day I heard the lifeguards muttering about dealing with "this Voulet or Toulet." But they never bagged Lyle for the prank, one of his more innocent.

Lyle used his chemistry set to produce "rotten-egg smell," his own description. He would trick you into sniffing this stuff, and as you gagged and caught your breath, he would say, "fucking reeks doesn't it?" I remember Mr. Goulet yelling at Lyle to stop making "that goddam shit smell." But he didn't. One day Lyle whipped up a batch, smuggled it into the Dairy Bar, and stuck it up in front of the fan, which wafted fumes through the place. It stunk up the joint so bad that Bud Fuller made everybody wait outside. Lyle watched from down the street, laughing his ass off. They found the stuff and threw it out but never traced it to Lyle, though I'm sure they had their suspicions. Mr. Goulet could have told them, and probably would have, such was his distaste for the shit smell. Bud Fuller actually got off easy. He should have been thankful the Dairy Bar was not a proving ground for another of Lyle's projects.

I'm not sure what chemicals he used, but Lyle manufactured a potent explosive and packed it into empty carbon dioxide capsules made of soft metal, the kind they use in pellet guns. "Grenades," he called them, with good reason. One blew apart someone's tree fort out in Rankin Bush. Another time he put one in a model car and left it on top of a baseball dugout in Central Park, topped with heavy-gauge galvanized metal. The blast put a dent in the roof and shattered the wood below. Lyle found pieces of the toy car on the other side of the park.

It truly amazes that nobody got maimed by one of these, or by the firecrackers that anybody could buy, especially the four-inch cannons, which practically qualified as munitions. Over by the IGA, near the mulberry tree,

I once saw someone put one of these in his back pocket and light it. It blew the ass right out of his jeans. I wonder how he explained that.

Roger Goulet, Lyle's older brother, was a prodigious swearer. When working on his car, it seemed that he began every sentence with "goddam fucking," followed by a certain engine part, distributor, starter, solenoid, whatever, that was failing to cooperate. Lyle was great at imitating these outbursts. When not so engaged, Roger was a smooth raconteur and I remember him telling the Dairy Bar crowd about the 1960 Olympics. He and Wayne knew judo, which Wayne had been taught at the deaf school, and had watched this judo event, in which this "seven-foot Jap," Roger said, apparently mopped up on some smaller opponent. Roger was supposed to be a tough guy too, with real fast boots, but I never heard of him mixing it up. As far as swearing he was rivaled by Ron Livermore, who lived a few blocks over, near Central Park.

Ron had that classic greasy-haired juvenile delinquent look, and often sported a toothpick. I sometimes hung around with his younger brother Don and when I went over there one day Ron was on the couch singing along to "Be My Baby" by the Ronettes. Before Don could leave, Ron asked him if he had cleaned the house. Don said he had cleaned his room and part of the place. This got Don up off the couch as though jabbed with a cattle prod, and he went off on him in colorful terms, at high volume.

For his part, Don deployed a favorite phrase, derived from a brand of cigarette, Noblesse, whose slogan was "noblesse oblige." Don was not the first to call these cigs "nob-less," but he was the champ at using it as an insult. "Hey, nob-less, just shut up okay?" And everyone called cigarettes "fags," though even then you heard references to "cancer sticks," and of course "smokes."

The propaganda of the time, of course, portrayed smoking as endlessly cool, and it seemed as though everybody on television and in the movies smoked, so the tobacco commercials hardly constituted much of a change. "Take a puff and it's springtime," said the ads for Salem cigarettes. The Newport brand touted "a hint of mint," which kids changed to "a hint of shit." Winston ads claimed that "Winston tastes good like a cigarette should." Other ads of the time had kids singing along. These included, "Mabel, Black Label! There goes that call again for Carlings Black Label Beer."

Some parents responded to bad language by washing kids' mouths out with soap. This never happened to me and I doubt it proved very effective. Today they would likely jail any parent who tried it, just as the flatulent Mr. Dugal might get some grief for subjecting his kids to the "Dutch oven" treatment.

Centershot

Across Dougall from Woolco, on Nottingham Street, stood a place called the Elder Warehouse, though I never found out what wares were actually housed there. A gentleman known simply as "old man Elder," lived in a residence on the premises and drove a very nice Cadillac, a silver 1959, the one with the sweeping tailfins, each bearing a pair of bullet taillights, a model calculated to enrage Ralph Nader, who decried Detroit's phallic designs. One night Bob "Poojie" Olteen, Dave Drayton and one other guy, Ron something from another part of town, took it for a joyride and duly smashed it up over by the highway 401 overpass or maybe on Dougall. Those were the days before seat belts, which they probably would not have worn anyway, and Poojie shot through the windshield. The resulting scars on his forehead gave him a fierce look. The three got some kind of probation, but the heist was big news at the time.

Poojie's nickname derived from "pudgy," his condition as an infant. He was a car enthusiast who once tried to organize a club called the Pacers. He lived right behind Leo Ferri's Shell station on Dougall, where he could sometimes be found. The guys who worked there had built some incredible machines. My favorite was a white 1955 Chevrolet, owned by Kenny Hebert, all jacked up in front to allow the headers to emerge above the front wheels. These could be capped off for street driving, a more sophisticated version of the "cutouts" some guys rigged to their exhaust, emerging behind the front wheel. A tachometer had been mounted on the dashboard, and the transmission sported a Hearst shifter, the one praised in all the hot-rod magazines. I was in awe of this car but never talked to the owner. It's hard to exaggerate the power these vehicles held over us.

One day in front of Woolco I ran into Don Torchin, who was staring intently at a red Oldsmobile convertible in the parking lot.

"That car gives me a hard-on," he said. It was indeed a sexy machine, especially in red. But maybe Don, who was on the heavy side, needed to get out more.

Poojie inherited a 1948 Indian motorcycle, though not in running condition. Though occasionally on the prickly side, he tolerated kids of my age and the two of us worked hours making head gaskets and torqueing down the cylinder head. We pushed the thing, very heavy and awkward, and popped the clutch. It made some encouraging noises but never fired up. Poojie later told me he rolled the bike into the Detroit River but I think he traded it for something else, maybe some tools. It would be worth big money today, in any condition.

Motorcycles and cars commanded our attention, but we did not neglect the thriving railway system. On the other side of Dougall, back of Alpine Nursery, the railyards stretched along Howard Avenue. Many a summer day we could be found here hopping trains, which was easy to do. They were rolling slow at that point, so you jumped on and rode for about a quarter mile, then got off and did it again. We could have stayed on and rode to who knows where, but there were other places to explore.

To one side, near Howard, loomed a concrete railroad tower, long abandoned. It became something of a hideout and we would slide down its loading chute, probably once used for coal, and climb on its rusty ladders. It was a good three stories high, topped by an office, windows smashed out, with an old desk, books and other junk. One day we went up there and found that someone had written on the door:

YOU ARE BEING WATCHED BOYS

This deterred us not at all. In fact, we thought it was pretty funny. Watched by whom? Danny Thomas? Marilyn Monroe? Zorro? Mr. Mansfield? Nobody ever detained us in the rail yards.

One day I was there with Johnny Maxwell, Don Livermore and Mark Lantz, who was singing what was then a hit tune by Chubby Checker, about a dance called the Popeye. The first line went "Pop, Pop, Pop-eye." Mark changed the first line to "Fuck, fuck, Popeye." This prompted Johnny Maxwell to respond "I'd much rather fuck Olive Oil." It was all rather crude, but he had a point. About this time, Ray Stevens ("Ahab the Arab") had on one album a song about Popeye, which noted that Olive had a color television, and that Popeye would hurt you if you messed with her. Bluto found out the hard way. As the song said, Popeye made a mess out of Bluto's "countenance."

Johnny was rail thin and his skin burned easily so he wore long-sleeved shirts even in summer. Like his older brother Tom, he was glib and sarcastic, known as a "funny" guy, which it was good to be. But we were all glib and sarcastic. To be the target of that sarcasm, all you had to do was look or act different than the general group.

If you did this, you made a "centershot" of your self, something you definitely did not want to be. And you were "centered out," which you didn't ever want to happen, under any circumstances. I remember my friends explaining that some incident, in class or otherwise, had left them feeling "totally centered out." A certain style of clothing or shoes, even if you liked it, might be rejected because wearing it would center you out.

For example, a local kid named Larry Tiller went over to Detroit and bought a pair of those black and white patent leather wing-tip shoes, the type that might be found on a Brush Street pimp.

"Are you going to wear those shoes to the dance?" someone asked Larry.

"No," he said. "They're nice shoes and I don't want to wreck them."

Those shoes centered out Larry Tiller, who also wore a white T-shirt with a pocket to the dance. A more notable centershot case involved John Hartloff, one of my Glenwood schoolmates.

John and his older brother Rolf were from Germany. Paul Adams once called John a "Nazi," and Mr. Mansfield, the principal really yelled at him for it, something about "turning back history to criticize a person." John's father, according to him anyway, had been opposed to Hitler. This might have been true but one would want to look into it. At my high school in Essex, for example, the principal was Werner Franke, who had been a submarine commander for the Third Reich. A lot of parents didn't like it at the time. My father, who spent the duration of the conflict in the Merchant Marine, would have been a prime target for Franke's torpedoes, but he never said anything.

One day John Hartloff showed up at Glenwood school wearing lederhosen and one of those German hats. He looked like the singers in the opening chorus of "Springtime for Hitler" in *The Producers*. Shorts of any kind would have centered him out but this was too much. John got more attention than if he had showed up for class naked, or in a clown suit. Well, maybe not quite, but he never again dared to wear lederhosen to school. I doubt whether anyone has attempted to duplicate his feat.

Some years later, at a summer church camp out in the county, we discussed the morality of the topless bathing suit, which had just appeared on the scene but not yet a big seller. One girl rather proudly proclaimed that she saw nothing wrong with the topless bathing suit, that the human body, created by God, was nothing to be ashamed of, and so on. Someone asked if she would therefore wear a topless bathing suit.

"No," she snapped. "I am not going to make a centershot out of myself."

Her name now escapes me but if she had put on the topless suit it would not have made her a big attraction.

People would plot to center someone out. At Teentown dances, Rick Michalski, would come up beside someone who was dancing oddly, hold his hand high in the air and point down at them, sometimes adding "centershot!" Though nasty, it could be worse.

"Suckhole," another popular insult, packed even more of a sting. This one could be classed as fighting words. "Hey *suck*hole," someone would say. "Where'd you get that stupid shirt."

Sandals were also perpetually out. Mark Lantz saw this one guy wearing them and said, "Hey kid, this ain't Jerusalem. We don't wash feet here."

Like clothes, insults were subject to fads. For a time it was fashionable to call someone a "tool" as in "what a *tool*." I also heard someone dubbed a "toolbox," a term I thought might be local but which I heard in Vancouver some years later, in the same context. Tool might have been vaguely sexual, like calling someone a "prick," also common and, for a time, "wick," as well as "wing-wong." For a while the in-word was "dink," as in "Hey Torchin, you big dink." People would also say "how's your doof?" or "how you hangin'?" or "don't let your meat loaf."

Kids who kept their hands in their pockets were considered to be playing with themselves, more specifically, playing "pocket pool." Mark Lantz was once caught in this activity and asked what the score was. "I don't know," he said, "but the referee's a prick." If a kid left his fly open, he would be told he was "flying low."

There was also at Glenwood a student of German extraction named Dick Mueller, and we found out his real name was Wolfgang. This then became a taunt. "Hey, Wolfgang!" people would say, to center him out. Dick was doubtless annoyed, but didn't let on. And in any case, he wasn't much into the social scene.

Shake 'em Down at Teentown

The Teentown dances, part of that scene, were held in the gym at Southwood School, also the site of some supervised pick-up basketball games on week nights. The Hannans and guys like Pete McNab played there. We used to give the teams stupid names like "Wires," etc. While waiting to play one night, McNab and I were goofing around on the stage and got tossed.

At Southwood, this big guy named Alan Pinch was the prevailing heavy. Danny Napier, nicknamed "Scraper," also went there. But the dances at Glenwood or Christ the King were similar, very seldom with a live band, though at one early Glenwood dance the Royal Whirls performed, a pantomime group with John Tregaskiss, Barry Campbell and John Watson. "Duke of Earl," was one of their tunes, and another one with a line about "he was a bad motorcycle," with a lot of ba-bop-ba-bas in it. They put on a great show.

Barry was one of the taller kids in the hood, gangly but stylishly dressed – a "sharp dresser" as we used to say – well groomed, with a prominent Adam's apple. He was a good basketball player, though he liked to shoot much more than pass, a habit that sometimes ran afoul of Mr. Hinch. Now that I think of it, most of us preferred to shoot rather than pass. I remember Barry walking through the hall at Glenwood school and in his deep voice singing "Get a Job," by the Silhouettes. "Dip, dip, dip, dip, werp, wa werp werp werp, get a job. Sha-na-na-na na," and so on. Mr. Hinch ordered him to stop.

The best musician of the group was John Watson, also something of a lady's man. John had been linked romantically to Kathleen Jones and the two had reportedly been interrupted during the course of some compromising acts. This kind of tale was usually beyond verification. A lot of the lore about girls was all lies, and some locals were known as fabulous bullshitters.

One would reportedly talk about popping a wheelstand with his parents' Cadillac, which even defied the laws of physics. He bragged about drinking 30 beers at the Riviera, picking up five broads and screwing them all in one night. And so on. Maybe the stories were exaggerated, but this fellow's initials were in fact BS, an example of what William Blake called fearful symmetry. At least Bob Offen did not have BO. This guy was indeed full of bullshit.

A disc jockey usually prevailed at the dance, spinning the hits and fielding requests announcing snowballs, ladies' choice etc. After one dance at Glenwood, one of the Dairy Bar hard-rocks threatened to beat up the DJ, who was, as we used to say, "scared shitless" and "shitting bricks." Some people just hung out or walked around but most danced. I'm not sure how they came about, but the dances were of local creation.

One was called, of all things, the California, and best performed to a tune called "I Remember Carol," by Tommy Boyce, which had a good dancing beat and some clapping in it, an assessment that sounds like what Dick Clark used to elicit from teenagers on "American Bandstand," which everybody watched. The California was a group dance, something like what is now called line dancing. Everybody went through a series of shuffling steps while standing on one spot, first with the right foot then left. Then you kicked twice, turned 90 degrees and shuffled three steps back and clapped, followed by a sliding motion to one side, then back again. Then you turned another 90 degrees and started it all over again. Or something like that. Turn, turn, kick turn and so on. It was pretty easy and we would have 20 people doing this at one time. Doubtless it would look lame now but at the time it was a blast. Another favorite tune for the California was "You Can't Sit Down," by the Dovells.

As Chubby Checker said about the Pony, any way you do it, you're gonna look real fine. The California constituted our "big boss line." As for "I'll Remember Carol," it must have been only a local hit because in my travels I never met anyone who had heard of it. No great loss.

"The Locomotion," by Little Eva, prompted a chain set up, something that had been done on TV, a chugging motion like a railroad train, as Eva sang it. We all thought she was a babe.

In the "Chalypso" another local step, two lines face each other and shuffled back and forth. Anybody could do it. The favorite accompaniment for the Chalypso was anything by the Four Seasons, "Sherry," "Rag Doll," and "Walk Like a Man" and "The Gypsy Cried," by Lou Christie, another falsetto crooner.

Of course, the twist, mashed potatoes and jerk were also popular, along with the fly, the monkey, the pony, the hully gully – after the Dovells' tune – the shing-a-ling, and the boogaloo, all with their particular gyrations. One could look "real fine," as Chubby Checker said, in any one of these. Jimmy Dugal, while not generally known as a dancer, was great at the boogaloo.

Certain tunes were guaranteed to get people up, particularly "Do You Love Me?" by the Contours, which began with a recited verse backed by a plaintive trill on guitar, almost like a mandolin. Then it really rocked out.

Another favorite was "Shake Shake Sherry," by the Flairs, with verses punctuated by "abomomalom, a bomalomalom," typical nonsense syllable glossalalia. This was more of a national hit, unlike "Mind Over Matter," by Nolan Strong, which charted locally. Nolan Strong was a talented guy who pissed a lot of people off by failing to show for a concert in Detroit. Jamie Coe, also out of Detroit had a local hit with "The Fool," a man who told his baby goodbye, and came to regret it. He sure wasn't the first, and certainly not the last.

A crooner named Matt Lucas also scored locally with "I Want to Move," which was actually a 12-bar blues, with train sound effects. The singer wanted to move down to "that good lovin' land." Little Stevie Wonder's "Fingertips" always got the joint moving, as did the offerings of the girl groups, "One Fine Day," by the Chiffons and above all "Dancing in the Street" by Martha and the Vandellas, in which lead singer Martha Reeves says "can't forget the motor city." The Four Tops, a Detroit group, appeared at dances in Windsor. Bob Seger and the Last Herd scored a local hit called "Heavy Music."

The first line asked if you listened to the radio when the big bad beat comes on. As it happens, we did, and not to just any station.

The 30 or so Detroit radio stations included WKNR, WCAR, WJBK, and WXYZ, with Joel Sebastian and Lee Allen, "on the horn," who closed his show with "I Can't Get Started," by Frank Sinatra. In the early 1960s these stations met their match with Windsor's 50,000-Watt CKLW, a powerhouse that covered 27 states and six provinces, regularly got calls from New York and Philadelphia, and was once even picked up in New Zealand. Chicago stations would follow CKLW's lead. Recording artists such as the Four Tops, the Temptations, Stevie Wonder, Bob Seger, Dionne Warwick, Mitch Ryder and others quickly grasped that if CKLW played their record, it stood a good chance of scoring a national hit. They would duly show up at CKLW studios, right on the Windsor waterfront, but that was not enough. Their record had to be approved by the station's music director, Rosalie Trombley.

She was from nearby Leamington, the "tomato capital of Canada," and CKLW hired her as a switchboard operator before promoting her to the music library and then musical director. She reportedly boasted the "best ears in the business" but didn't like everything she heard. She told one manager point blank that his client's song was "a piece of shit." That kind of candor once earned her a death threat. Bob Seger even wrote a song about her, "Rosalie." He sings about "everybody's favorite little record girl," noting that "she's got the tower, she's got the power."

That was true. Rosalie did have the power and CKLW had the tower. That's why Burton Cummings and the Guess Who ("American Woman") drove all the way from Winnipeg to take her to lunch. Tony Orlando, Alice Cooper and others credit Rosalie and CKLW with launching their success. She recommended that Elton John go with "Benny and the Jets," not "Candle in the Wind," if he wanted to crack the R&B market, and he took her advice.

Robin Seymour, another local, had a television show, "Swingin' Time," broadcast from CKLW studios. Jim Ouellette and myself once tried to walk onto a show, when the special guest was Troy Shondell, whose only hit was "This Time," that mournful thing with the heavy organ that sounds like the ones they play at hockey games. They wouldn't let us in but we came close.

Dave Drayton, Rick Michalski, and Don Torchin, three of the coolest locals, part of the "in" group, improvised a step called the "DRD," for Dave, Rick and Don, though it sounds like some government agency. This dance didn't really catch on but I remember Dave Gratton showing me how to do it, while singing, "Come on, baby, let's do the DRD." Dave was an aspiring musician who once tried to play with Larry Roy, who put his guitar back in the case and walked out when Rick proved unable to play a G chord. Dave's older brother Rick, though not very big, was a more athletic type, and could often be found at the Dairy Bar. He also enjoyed success with the ladies.

To avoid being a centershot one generally dressed up for local dances. Style definitely came before comfort and the unspoken dress code included tight black pants, called "blades," appropriately enough, which had often been stitched even tighter by Clem Gaudette's mother, an excellent seamstress whose house bordered West Grand near the Grand Marais Ditch. You bought the pants 14 inches or so around the bottom and for a few bucks she would taper them down to 13 or even 12 inches. Getting them on and off was murder, particularly for me, even though some of the pants had a slot on the side of about three inches that facilitated entry and exit. I had size 12 feet from the time I was 12, which led to some kidding. People would say I could probably swim well underwater, or that I'd be taller if I wasn't bent underneath so much. Nobody likes to be ridiculed and I tried to squeeze into shoes too small for me. My feet still show the effects of this habit.

Clem Gaudette had a shock of dark hair and thick brows, and was always going somewhere on his balloon-tire bike. People would generally approach Clem first about "taking in" the pants. He played in the local softball league and I recall he was pretty good.

At dances the guys wore white shirts with those tabs on the collar that held up your tie, in those days a narrow, dark job, often with some kind of clip. The really stylish types wore these blazers with a belt at the back, two buttons on each side, that served no purpose other than to be there, and to signify that the wearer was "in." Jack Girty, a big-time dancer, had one of these, and so did Rick Michalski, probably the most athletic dancer of the bunch. Slow dancing was another matter.

My favorite tune for this activity was "Sixteen Candles" by the Crests. I also liked "Talk To Me," by Sonny and the Sunglows, "Since I Don't Have You," by the Skyliners, and "Any Day Now," by Chuck Jackson, a guy who really had soul, a quality very important to us. Some popular tunes weren't suitable for any kind of dancing. For example, "Telstar," this pretentious organ thing with a vocal accompaniment at the end that made it sound like the theme from Star Trek. And a tune like that one about flowers on the wall, playing solitaire till dawn, with a deck of 51, smoking cigarettes and watching Captain Kangaroo, well that was a novelty, like "Tie Me Kangaroo Down, Sport." People could also be found singing "Does your Chewing Gum Lose its Flavor," by Lonny Donegan. It had the ring of some British drinking song, or maybe a show tune from some farce. For a few years novelty tunes like "Purple People Eater," and "The Monster Mash," were the rage.

"Sixteen Candles" was a hit for the Crests, a group I had never seen but which I now know from watching old footage on infomercials to be composed of blacks and whites. The Marcels, who sang that up-tempo version of "Blue Moon" with all the bom-ba-boms in it, were also black and white. The group that sang "The Book of Love," I thought was all white but they turned out to be all black. As noted, I thought the Tokens, who sang "The Lion Sleeps Tonight," were all black but were all white. When it came to music, we were all colorblind. We wanted good music and didn't care where it came from. The same held true in sports.

My favorite boxer was Floyd Patterson, and I was absolutely devastated when Ingemar Johansen knocked him out. But Floyd came back to defeat the Swede twice, before getting clocked by Cassius Clay, which happened to many boxers, black and white, even before Clay became Muhammad Ali. He was another guy we liked, a big-mouth and a show-off to be sure, but one who could back it up, and did. In our hood, it was okay to talk the talk as long as you could walk the walk.

Our interest in sports, however, often took a back seat to interest in girls, which had started long before.

It's What's Up Front That Counts

The first girl who really knocked my socks off was Linda Matson, who lived on Mark Ave. She was dark-haired and dark-eyed, with long lashes and this great beauty mark on one cheek. In fact, she once invited me to kiss her right there, but that was as far as it went. I think their family "moved away," as we used to say. We never thought it enough to say they "moved," though we might have used that if they bought a different house in the same area.

I was also taken with Pamela Edmonds, a blue-eyed blond who was the daughter of my softball coach. Trouble was, Bob Buncick had dibs on Pam. Linda Gasparini, in my class at Glenwood, also attracted my attention, but Bill Pengelly claimed her. I liked Sharon Kendall, a newcomer to the school, but the feeling, unfortunately, wasn't mutual. I got along with Lois Shouldice, nicknamed "Shoelace," a pleasant and intelligent girl whose parents ran a motel on Huron Line.

That road, which becomes Highway 3, is a major artery with a number of businesses, hangouts and eateries. These included the Sandhill House, near Grand Marais, and Luigi's Spaghetti House, a place I never entered but which was rumored to be a whorehouse, which we pronounced "hoor house." I'm sure there was nothing to it and that Luigi's was not, in fact, a hoor house. The rumor might have had something to do with a red light on the sign, supposedly a dead giveaway. In a variation on the mispronunciation, locals would also attempt to be daring and funny in class with a mock cough that went "a-hoor, a-hoor."

My first regular slow-dance partner was Betty Jane Smith, a year older and who had previously always danced with an even older guy who wore these striped college-type sweaters that stayed in style for a few years. Betty Jane wore braces but I didn't care. After one dance, Bob Cushman commented that they had seen me with that girl "with the silver smile." Betty lived on Dougall, in an older two-story house across from Ashton's Motel. We weren't an item for very long. We weren't exactly "going around," a stage between friends and going steady.

Lynn Summers, who had been going around with Mark Lantz, gave new meaning to "slow" dancing. She tended to hang on tight. She wore her hair up, like the girl groups of the time, but not in the "ratted" style. She lived close by and we liked each other, but it never seemed to work out.

I had a bad habit of falling hard for older girls like Claudia Reaume – no relation to Fats and Leonard that I knew of – and Pat Meredith, whom I saw quite a bit because I was friends with her brother Steve. Pat had these beautiful green eyes and always a dark tan in summer, though she used this tanning junk, probably Tanfastic, an actual brand name of the time, that gave the skin a kind of deep orange hue. Man Tan was another popular product that yielded mixed results. But whatever the shade, girl's shorts were short then and you got to see a lot of the tan. Such brevity was the theme of "Short Shorts" by the Royal Teens, which included Al Kooper, later of Blood Sweat and Tears.

I sensed that Pat liked me too and Steve confided in me that his sister had told him that if we had been the same age it would have been a lock. That did a lot for my confidence, I'll tell you. One of Pat's favorite songs was "Will You Still Love Me Tomorrow," by the Shirelles and co-written by Carole King. When you went over there, Pat would be singing along to it.

Claudia Reaume was on the short side but had large breasts, which made dancing with her an adventure. Her younger sister Michelle, though not similarly equipped, was prettier, and my age, but always had a boyfriend. She worked for a while in the record department at Woolco. We changed the lettering on the hit-parade chart when she wasn't there, though I'm sure she "got shit for it," as we used to say.

Chris Gatrall, a much pursued local beauty, could have starred with Lynn Summers and Claudia Reaume in something called *Terms of Endowment*, with top billing. Veterans of the hood will recall that she deployed these really big breasts, of the magnitude that gets them called "pontoons" and so on. You could actually see them from behind, and you noticed that Chris didn't make a lot of sudden movements. She was entirely capable of giving any guy, at any time, "a rise in his Levis." Mark Lantz also used to say of Chris, in a mock English accent, "check the pectorals on that one," or "rather nice pecks."

Large breasts rated a girl very high at that time, the Pre-Silicone Era, and the hey-day of Marilyn Monroe, Jayne Mansfield, Sophia Loren, Gina Lollobrigida and other screen goddesses. In accord with this reality, we adapted an ad for Winston cigarettes that said "It's what up front that counts." Lucky Strike also had a slogan, LSMFT, "Lucky Strike means fine tobacco," which we adapted to "Loose straps means floppy tits," and "leaky Sheiks means future twins."

The term "condom" was not used in those days and people simply said Ramseys or Sheiks, the brand names. As legend had it, you could flash secret hand signals at a drug store if you wanted to buy these items but didn't want to say so out loud, with other customers around. I don't know who composed it, but this poem made the rounds:

In days of old, when knights were bold
And Sheiks were not invented
They slapped a sock around a cock
And babies were prevented

I don't recall ever talking to Chris Gatrall but I knew her sister Lynn, not of the same pectoral prowess but to my mind prettier. She was going around with Tommy Hannan and I remember hanging out with them at parties at the Reaume's house. Mr. and Mrs. Reaume had rules against what was then called necking, but we broke those rules, along with many others. Couples entangled in long mostly above-the-waist sessions that could leave the male participant with a case of "lover's nuts." Both parties could emerge with hickeys, the body art of the time. These could be strategically placed to escape detection but if you got one you could also flaunt it.

Girls like Chris were described as "stacked," and any speculation of whether she wore falsies never arose in Chris's case. Any fool could tell it was "all her." This could have been verified, of course, by "feeling her up," a popular activity reflected in a joke: Why don't girls have hair on their chest? Because grass doesn't grow on a playground. It was also possible, of course, to feel girls "down," if they would allow it. For their part, girls could conduct some exploratory maneuvers below the border and some did so with considerable enthusiasm. One even gained the nickname "stroker."

Other local babes included Judy Shields, a very sexy blond who lived on the other side of Huron Line and went to Cahill school. I think she had a brother, maybe Doug, reportedly a rowdy type. So was Judy, kind of a Tomboy, in addition to being a babe. Kenny Dagenais' older sister Donna was also a looker, but didn't hang out much and went out with older guys who had cars. Sharlene Lamarsh, who went to Northwood, was in Chris Gatrall's league and could always turn heads. It's what's up front that counts, and she had it, along with a "nice personality." Unfortunately, she was going steady with a guy who, Sharlene said, already had a drinking habit as a teenager. Once at a party, at Dave Pilkington's house, she complained to me about having a boyfriend who "gets pissed." April and Crystal Lake, who lived near Central Park, always had guys chasing after them. Karen Locke, who lived near Woolco, did not lack for attention. She looked a bit like Linda Malec, who lived not far from the Dairy Bar. Margaret Cornfoot, another pretty blond, also deserves mention.

Girls who were unattractive also got described in creative ways, as "scrags" or "hags." Sometimes "scurvy" would be part of it, or "scuzzy." These recall a line in *Harper*, in which Paul Newman says that being with this one woman is "like cuddling up to a piece of fungus."

Mark Lantz said of one girl that "I wouldn't take her to a worm fight." Warnings went out that before mixing it up with certain girls, a guy should "tie a two-by-four to his ass" lest he fall in. The girls had their own phrases for boys who failed to measure up, as one local would find out.

Tone Pine

Whether one danced or not, the Teentown events provided a forum for showing how cool you were. Aldo Colatti, who lived over by Central Park, used to show up with wine on his breath, having apparently pillaged his parents' supply. He would come up to you, hold his face near yours and say "Whhhhhaat are you doing?" making sure you could catch a whiff of the booze. Those without access to booze tried to get a buzz by dropping aspirins into Coca-Cola. I never tried this but I can say with some authority that it doesn't work.

Aldo, meanwhile, was strong and a good fighter. People would sometimes test strength by locking hands, a "finger fight," and seeing if you could bend the other guy's wrist back and make him yield. Nobody wanted to take on Aldo, who reportedly worked some construction with his father.

There was a Jim Colatti, maybe spelled Coulatti, at Glenwood, who reportedly had scored big time with a girl I will call Julie Darren, an older Glenwood student whom I remember as short, with short skirts, a ratted, bee-hive hairdo, and a bad complexion, by no means uncommon then for girls or guys. Clearasil was a big seller, along with this guck that would simply cover up the pimples. Judy had a kind of seductive, come-on look and you expected her to say something like "new in town, sailor?" I remember Kenny Dakin, or maybe his brother Dennis, telling Julie in the schoolyard, "Hey Julie, Jimmy Colatti was just here and said he wants to screw you." She shot back something like, "Yeah? Well what am I supposed to do about it, daddy-o?"

The Dakins also lived on McKay, and like their neighbors the Hannans were on the small side but good athletes. I remember one of them singing along to "Michael Rowed the Boat Ashore." That kind of Kingston Trio "folk" material had a following then, though most of us considered it corny, weak, and not very soulful.

The girl with the wildest reputation, whose name would be immediately apparent to any Central Park veteran, was not a great looker but "built like a brick shithouse," as people would say. This daring young lady had an entrepreneurial streak and would reportedly let you squeeze her tits for a small fee. More famously, she supposedly "took on" six guys in the Central Park dugouts, Dave Drayton among them. This same girl reportedly had a "crooked twat," an arrangement in which her sexual apparatus was supposedly off center by an inch or so. This crazy notion was likely evidence that nobody, in fact, had inspected the reproductive gear at close range. One claimed to have done so. The specific activity he described recalled a joke then making the rounds about the difference between the American rabbit and the French rabbit. The American rabbit goes hippity-hop. The French rabbit, on the other hand, goes lickety split.

The girl in question had an older brother who didn't seem much involved in the neighborhood but had a reputation as a tough guy. That was also true of many others I never saw throw down. Another bad-ass, on the large side and from across town, was this cat who called himself "Jingles," the name doubtless based on the character Andy Devine played on the Roy Rogers television show. I had a run-in with him many years later, based on something I had supposedly said to a girl he knew, but I still don't know his real name. I won't say he's fat, but when he steps on a cigarette that sucker is out.

In those times fat people did not believe they had special rights and did not blame fast-food chains for making them fat. But they still took a lot of grief. I forget who it was but one kid used to get asked: "Where do you buy your clothes? Windsor Tent and Awning?" Kids would also say, in the voice of a television announcer, "Want to lose ten pounds of ugly fat? Cut off your head." There were also references to Bimbo the baby elephant, I believe from the movie *Circus Boy*, though it might have been television.

Another kid who took a lot of grief was Robin Conn, a rather amorphous, awkward youth, whose parents owned Conn's Flowers. He was like Tommy Durocher in that he pulled his pants up so high you thought he might choke himself. When Robin started smoking the overall effect was even worse.

Though some of the phrases we used were mysterious, it was possible to track the origin of others. A local television show, "Milky's Party Time," with Milky the Clown, was sponsored by Twin Pines Dairies. Milky would perform some trick and get the kids to say the magic word, "Twin Pines." One time this kid, very loud, and obviously proud of himself, said "tone pine!" The story got big laughs for a long time and "tone pine" became a popular catchphrase, something you would say for no reason, just to show you were in the know. I believe someone even considered naming his cat Tonepine. Mark Lantz even reversed it and said something that sounded like "pay tay." Another popular catchphrase was "smock smock," but I don't know how it got started.

Mark hung out with Bob Kerr, whose real name, reportedly, was Robert Constantine. His hair was almost pure white, and his cheek bore a strange kind of birth mark. He was always around the Dairy Bar and liked to drink grape soda. "I'm just dying for some grape," he would say. Bob was a bit older, and a wannabe of sorts with the Dairy Bar regulars. He lived near Third Concession and his family situation, as I recall, was not very stable, a rarity in the neighborhood. Bob would describe to me in great detail the kind of car he wanted, a black 1957 Chevrolet convertible, with dual quads and of course dual exhausts. He hadn't decided on a column or floor shift, or bench seats versus bucket seats. The issue was whether the floor shift and bucket seats would allow his girlfriend to sit as close as he would like. And in those days the girls sat pretty close.

Bob went to Christ the King school, with baseball diamonds out back that hosted the local softball league. He didn't play in those, but I did.

The prevailing team was Standard Equipment Co., with pitcher Morley Foster, usually known as Moe Foster, and Wade Renaud at first base. The terror of the senior league was Dave Brooks, a tall fireballer who terrified batters, spectators and umpires, who needed to have their cup, mask and chest protector firmly in place when Dave Brooks took the mound. Another pitcher who didn't look that athletic but who could really wheel it was Gary Nosanchuk. I think his family had a construction business and I remember seeing a sign Nosanchuk-Buttery. A common sign around town was DAAPCO, Dinsmore Asphalt Paving Company, perpetually at work repaving Windsor's potted streets.

The diamonds at Christ the King were back-to-back with a junior and senior game going at once and pitchers warming up at the side of the backstop. Paul Adams played for a senior team sponsored by Zenith Electric. Their jerseys were purple, with gold letters and a lightning-bolt logo.

I managed to get on the John Madden team – no relation to the football commentator. They ran some kind of body shop or auto repair place. The squad promptly changed its sponsorship to Wansbrough's Sport Shop, run by Frank Wansbrough, who later became mayor of Windsor. I was in that shop one day when Leonard Reaume came in there and bought a shotgun.

The Wansbrough uniforms were silver with red letters. We were a middle-of-the-road team but we all had a blast. The coach was Mr. Edmonds, Pam's dad, and Mr. King. I remember him telling me not to swing at a pitch high and outside. I swung anyway and hit the ball into the right-center gap for a home run. I remember the pitcher, Bobby Richards, who had an older brother, Ronny, with a wicked curve ball he would showcase when we played "strikeout," by chalking a square on the wall of the Glenwood gym. If you let the pitch go and it hit in the square it was a strike. We used a tennis ball for this contest. Ronny would throw a curve that looked like it was coming right at your head then break into the zone.

In softball I also remember being struck out by Gary Johnson, a smooth, accurate pitcher, and by Charlie Berge, with a change-up that I should have seen coming because he telegraphed it with a smile. Ken Havens, the catcher, signaled the pitch. Kenny knew I liked to swing for the fences. They sure fooled me.

I pitched myself, with not much success or control. I would get behind in the count and had to forgo the windmill style for a simple underhand delivery, swung from behind the back to get momentum. But I wasn't as bad as Brian Menard, a real wild man who once pitched a ball clear over the backstop at Christ the King. He also walked three batters to load the bases then gave up a home run. He felt so bad about it he cried. Thereafter, when Menard pitched he would face taunts of "Tiny Tears," after a popular doll of the time that would actually cry, a partner for Chatty Kathy.

The good players on Wansbrough were Paul Soulliere and Bob Buncick, a fast base runner partly due to spikes, which gave him great traction for rounding the bases. I didn't have spikes and had to slow up to make the turn, once causing Bob, who was behind me, to be thrown out. Mr. Edmonds was really pissed, but I was going as fast as I could. Despite my lapses, I was known as a decent hitter. I remember Bobby Richards' dad, who coached, motioning the fielders to back up when I came to the plate. It was his team that I victimized with my homer. We won 19-3 that day, which Mr. Richard doubtless remembered. He was the coach when I was selected to try out for the all-star team and did not pick me for the squad. I felt pretty bad about it at the time, convinced I was a better player than Jackie Lezhnar, probably spelled wrong, who was the last name called. He lived on Dominion, on the other side of Grand Marais, and would always tell these stories about "wolf spiders." The family was Polish and Jackie still spoke with an accent.

When I left softball for hardball Paul Adams accused me of chickening out, that senior softball was a tougher game. I think he was wrong. Our coach was Mr. Bouffort, Barb's dad, and his son Dean was on the team, which might have been sponsored by Hamel and Taylor shoes. I caught for Steve Crowe, a chunky kid who had perfected a great curve and drop-ball pitch that looked like it fell off a table. The all-star team from this league, which I did not make, got to play the Detroit Mohawks, a team that usually prevailed with ease against Windsor's best.

Our senior hardball league was called Mic-Mac, and they used the diamond at the far end of Central Park. Those guys could really play. I remember this spectator yelling "Hey umpire, where you from? South America?"

When games were in progress, they didn't like anybody sitting under that tree over by the St. Mary's fence. But there were other places to go and have fun.

On Golden Ponds

Near the rail yards spread an open field that had once been home to Kenilworth race track, where the hooves of Man O' War and other thoroughbreds had once thundered. The Devonshire racetrack had stood on the other side of Howard Ave, and a few traces of it remained, some rickety stands and rubble. Nearby, in a small spread of bush, I discovered Devonshire pond, an idyllic spot, something out of a Mark Twain novel, and probably part of an old estate. Rumor has it that the severed head of a woman once turned up here, but I have not been able to verify the story.

The pond was about 100 feet across and maybe eight feet deep in the middle, though kids preferred to say it was "over your head." We used to take screens and drag up crawfish, which we called "crayfish." The place was full of them and also teemed with frogs. During one of these hunts I managed to drop my father's hunting knife, which his father had made for him, into the water. It was a beautiful thing, with a piece of bone in the middle of the handle. A panic struck me, like that horrible feeling you get when you realize your wallet is missing. I managed to dredge it up, to my great relief. And to my surprise, the Devonshire pond was actually navigable.

Someone had fashioned a raft out of logs, plywood and scrap lumber, and everybody who came to the pond used it, pushing themselves around with a pole. That operation proved difficult in the deeper water. One day a group of kids I didn't know showed up with a small outboard motor and gas tank, and rigged this gear on the raft, which did have a kind of crude transom. They fired up the motor and roared around the pond kicking up quite a wake. They didn't invite me for a ride. The ostensible leader of the group was this freckled, red-haired kid who looked like a cross between the boy on the Skippy peanut butter jar and Elmo in the Dagwood comic strip. I saw him at other places in Windsor but never spoke to him. That day the redhead was trying to get his friend to go in the water, which he did not want to do.

"Don't," he said, then, after a pause, "fuck off."

"Okay," said redhead. "Don't fuck off."

They all laughed at this. The place was clearly theirs for the day and after a while I took off. Though I didn't go there that day I had two other aquatic options besides the Lake Erie beaches that were out of easy bicycle range and stinking with dead fish.

Across Huron Line, you could swim in the "Brickyard," some sort of foundation that had filled with water and remained so. It was a favorite with the Tregaskiss brothers. Kids also sought out Cowpaddy Lake, also known as Lake Foreskin, on Walker Road, near Highway 401.

Cowpaddy-Foreskin wasn't really a lake but a reservoir from which they had reportedly dug the earth for various overpasses and such. It covered about 10 acres, with a dirt peninsula jutting out in the middle, leaving the water shaped in a rough U. From this peninsula we would swim to the other side, which took some endurance. It was definitely over your head so there was no resting once you got started. The water was brown and completely opaque, so you didn't dive in. The bottom was so muddy it squished between your toes. This was likely the source of the name. I've never stepped in fresh cow shit, but I imagine it was like that. At this place we sometimes saw others, well into their teens and beyond, who came to drink and frolic with girls.

You could see evidence of that activity even if nobody was there, spent condoms and of course beer bottles and sometimes "dirty books." This was a place nobody was supposed to be, and you were always expecting to be rousted, but nobody ever came, certainly not the cops. It amazes how much we were left to our own devices in most situations. The place probably made a great ice rink but I never went there in winter. You got the feeling that, as with Devonshire pond, not everybody knew about it, and that was part of the fun. And as Paul LeMat put it in *American Graffiti*, we were generally, "having fun, as usual." In that quest, the adults catered to us.

Mrs. Shady Now

Rak 'n Snak, down at the end of Gateway plaza, debuted about the same time Woolco opened. The owners discovered that combining a poolroom with a restaurant was a risky concept. They were aiming for a kind of family atmosphere and they even made you tuck in your shirt. Jeans were frowned on. To play cost a penny a minute, which we thought kind of steep at the time. They hired this older guy, vaguely British, bespectacled and white haired, to hold forth over the tables. I forget his name but do remember that most players regarded him as an asshole, meaning that he wouldn't let us do or say anything we wanted. We were not the easiest group to supervise.

The eatery was sort of middle brow, and only a brick wall about waist high separated that area from the tables, apparently an attempt to make snooker a spectator sport. A family would be dining in some style when someone would miss a shot and cut loose something like "nice shot, dipshit" or worse. If you got ejected for this type of thing, they sometimes wouldn't let you back in for a while. Shooters got in the habit of saying things like "scrotum" when they missed. The asshole supervisor let that slide, unless the player yelled it out.

The game of choice was snooker but the really good players like Rick Michalski and Wayne Shaw played skittles, golf and other games that demanded position play. In a game of straight pool they really shined. One of the regulars was Mike Derbyshire, this red-headed guy who was a decent snooker player but would always give you a hard time. Mike, who purported to be a tough guy, had a thing for Karen Locke, who lived on Church Street, near the Thornhills. I remember seeing Karen walk by the Dairy Bar when one of the regulars was out front sitting on a fender. He swirled around and made a pretty suggestive move, kind of like an invitation, but Karen didn't see it.

John Dowhan was also a big-time snooker player, though not among the elite, and a guy who would bet on anything. He always seemed to be in some card game for high stakes, at least by our standards. He had pretenses of being a tough guy, but not as bad as Mike Derbyshire.

The Rak, as we called it, was an important gathering place, particularly on Fridays. People would meet there before going off to some dance or whatever. The flower pots outside made great sitting places, as well as a platform for impromptu speeches that sometimes astonished incoming shoppers. A nearby phone booth got heavy use, and I remember once waiting for an older guy to get out of there. He thought I was standing too close and really chewed me out, which I suppose I deserved.

Another stopping post and sometime hangout was Shady's, at the corner of Dougall and Cabana, near Roseland Golf Course. It was a mom-and-pop convenience store where Dennis Shady, one of the kids, worked the counter. He knew a lot of people so you would wind up talking to him, or his older brother. The family might have been Persian, and Mrs. Shady, sometimes lurking in the background at the store, found her way into a song.

The tune was "Wooden Heart," a 1961 hit by Joe Dowell that was actually a cover of a German song, *Muss I Denn*, which Elvis Presley sang in *G.I. Blues*. I found it corny and infantile, very un-Motown. As Edwin Starr said, he didn't have no kind of soul. Dowell's version had a section in German that said *Stadtele hinaus*, which Jim Ouellette duly replaced with "Mrs. Shady now." It caught on around the hood.

North on Dougall, toward downtown Windsor, Ashton's Motel offered other attractions. They had a store and lunch counter almost the same vein as the Dairy Bar, not as big but with a pinball machine. It was one of those baseball outfits, with these three narrow steel ramps you could used to launch balls into the stands. They key to success was holding the ball with the flippers, which allowed you to survey your options. Once you mastered this you could rack up free games with relative ease, and when you did the machine popped like a small firecracker. Several of us would be waiting to play, which gave us an excuse to stay in the place without simply loitering. We would buy chips and soft drinks but the real kicker was the magazine stand, directly adjacent to the pinball.

Ashton's carried *Playboy* and similar publications, which Dave Drayton was adept at slipping out and keeping by the side of the pinball, to be brought up for the occasional glance. If the proprietors, whom I guess were named Ashton, were hip to it they never let on. One could say it was the breast of times.

Farther down Dougall, toward downtown, and just before the Elmwood, stood the Dorwin Plaza, Windsor's first attempt at a mall, with a Sentry department store. Their slogan was "Sentry Guards Your Dollar" and their symbol some guy decked out like one of the Buckingham Palace guards. Woolco took away a lot of their business.

In the parking lot of this complex appeared something called the Jumpin' Jiminy Trampoline Club, nothing more than several trampolines, with a supposedly expert attendant who looked more like a carnival worker. You paid your money and took your chances. I got the first-level badge they handed out, a pretty cheesy thing it was too, compared to some of the other "crests" you got for baseball and so on. It didn't require much in the way of expertise but I never got the chance to advance.

The operation vanished overnight. I heard some kid had injured himself, which was probably inevitable. Those things really shot you into the air, and you didn't always land as intended. The owners decamped without a trace and that was the end of the Jumpin' Jiminy Trampoline Club.

A skeet range operated behind Dorwin Plaza, and kids would go there to pick up shotgun shells, essentially useless, but a cool thing to have in one's possession. On the other side of Dougall, next to the Rose Bowl, was Woodall's driving range where some kids would try to swipe golf balls. The purpose for this heist wasn't clear because few of us played the game. One who did was Derek Bennett, an owlish, scholarly type who thought the Dairy Bar crowd were complete thugs and idiots. Derek was always bringing practice balls to Curry Park and chipping around, sometimes getting chewed out by the park supervisor, whereupon he would move to St. Gabriel's field next door.

Derek's father drove a black 1958 Buick Special, an enormous four-door hard top with more chrome than I've ever seen on an automobile. I can't imagine that barge giving Don Torchin or anybody else a hard-on. But you could probably make a Volkswagen out of one fender.

"You ought to try golf," Derek told me, with a professorial air. "It's very relaxing."

I never progressed farther than chipping a few balls and I did not find it relaxing, another way of saying I was bad at it. I think Jeff Conrad gave it a try. He was a pudgy kid who hung around Curry Park and bragged how his father had taken him aside and told him about sex. I once heard him mocked as "birds-and-bees Conrad" but I doubt he was able to put the instruction to much use, at least for a while.

The Stanko family, who lived on McKay, also played golf in Curry Park. They all had rather big heads, the source of some cruel jokes. They got called "light bulb," for example. Mr. Stanko was a big-time bowler and the kids, especially Mike, excelled at golf, which we used to play in Curry Park. When the supervisor chased us out, we would go next door to St. Gabriels.

Mark Lantz and I used to ride our bikes to the Bowlero, on Tecumseh, on Saturday mornings, for league play. In the *Windsor Star* I used to actually keep track of the better bowlers like Tony Chibi, and this big curly-haired man, Pat something, maybe Pat Balint, who also worked at Bowlero and bowled for a team sponsored by the Bali-Hi Hotel on Ouellette. One year Tony Chibi was bowling for the national title but lost out to a Saskatchewan kegler named "Red" Glasser.

The trick was finding the same ball each week, not an easy task. You couldn't exactly hide it anywhere, and most balls were in bad shape or "baffed out," as kids would say. The best I ever scored was 158, the highest in the league that day, so I got a free hamburger. After the games we would bowl as long as they left the lanes on. The ride home was always an adventure, with no bike lanes to speak of. We would usually ride down Dominion rather than Dougall. We never got hit, something of a miracle. Nobody wore helmets and that was also true of most motorcyclists.

The primo bowler from our neighborhood was Wayne Dubs' father, who regularly scored more than 200. My father bowled down at the Grand Terrace, older lanes on Tecumseh, where all the pinboys hated him. He fired the ball so hard he would knock pins across two lanes. He later switched to the Rose Bowl on Dougall, which boasted 50 lanes.

Bud Lantz, Mark's father, was an occasional bowler and always jovial. "Lloyd," he once asked me, "are you a smart feller or just a fart smeller?" We thought this was pretty funny, especially coming from a grownup. Bud thought it was pretty funny too.

I remember Maurice Roy, Larry's father, explaining how a tire gauge worked. "You stick this up your ass," he said, "and when you fart, this comes out." Maurice ran a trucking business called Roy's Trucking, appropriately enough. They had this weasely little dog, Queenie. And Larry's sisters, Linda and Lorraine, used to tease me with taunts of "Lloyd the boyd, Lloyd the boyd." But Larry was a good friend and a fine musician. I remember him playing this piece called "The Gauchos" and "Guitar Boogie Shuffle."

Larry had a 78 rpm record of "True Fine Mama," by Little Richard, and some other tunes by that artist. My own collection included "C.C. Rider," by Chuck Willis, "Daddy's Home," by Shep and the Limelights, and "All Shook Up," by Elvis Presley. "Mr. Lee," by the Chordettes, was also in there somewhere. We spent a lot of time listening to records in Larry's basement, where we also assembled model cars. Many kids had built quite a collection of those. Larry lived at 3181 Dominion Boulevard, two houses away from Dave Jameson, who lived at the corner of Dominion and Norfolk, right across from Larry Howe.

Dave was taller than most of us, a kind of silent, quizzical type. He had pretty firm opinions and once dressed me down for saying that the song "Somewhere," from *West Side Story*, should be higher on the hit parade than it was.

"Everybody has their own opinions, Lloyd," he said. Yes, we did indeed.

I remember that Alfred Small, who lived on Longfellow, was a partisan of "Leave Me Alone," by Baby Washington. She was through with love, and couldn't take it any more. It was a ballad in the vein of "Don't Make Me

Over," by Dionne Warwick, which came out later. Neither Alfred Small nor Dave Jamison was very musical and neither played an instrument. The girls weren't much attracted to Dave. You got the feeling that the family was more religious than most, Baptists I think. His father, whose bald head had a shine to it, would answer the phone "greetings," as though he were singing.

Back then, "skinhead," was the term of choice for bald people. I don't think Dave's parents approved of me very much, just as my parents had their doubts about Lyle Goulet, hardly the only character in the neighborhood.

Paperboys and Convertibles

anny Snively I didn't know well but he had the reputation of a prankster, a kind of Dennis the Menace type. Pete Stoddard was known as a tough guy and looked the part, all sinewy and with a suspicious squint. He liked to hang around the rail yards and was in favor of forming a gang that would claim the yards as their exclusive turf, with a clubhouse in the old tower. It never happened.

The Longmores, Johnny and Ed, lived on Longfellow. I knew Johnny, who was older than me, because he also had a *Windsor Star* paper route and was very good at folding the papers into that neat tube that you could throw onto the porch – except with picky people who wanted you to tuck it inside the door. Those were the same people who never had any money when you went to collect. I hated that job. Gordie Moore always gave me a hard time and I was afraid of his Keeshond, a big one.

I worked with Paul Bradshaw, who used his newspaper bag as a shield to light his cigarette on windy days. When it snowed we pulled the papers along on one of those wooden sleds with thin metal rails. These also got used on the overpass, where Dougall turns into highway 401. If you didn't have a sled or toboggan you used cardboard or an inner tube. Some kids would build these ramps at the bottom that would send you flying. I heard a story about someone who tried to fly off this ramp standing up, an early attempt at snowboarding on a toboggan, but who wound up breaking a leg. Years later, Poojie confessed that it was him.

We all picked up our papers at the same place, the bridge over the Grand Marais Ditch at Academy Drive. The first step was to get the page count. Holiday editions made for some heavy lifting. Johnny Longmore, who had a long route, was a likeable guy, kind of a joker, and knowledgeable when you got to know him. He worked hard and had a sense of decorum. His older brother Ed, a short, curmudgeonly type, was usually pissed off about something. I don't remember seeing him smile, and he already looked old. He drove a motor scooter, which made him a joke to the Dairy Bar crowd, and of course to anyone in the Nomads. It was light blue, probably a Lambretta or Vespa, with faded paint. Ed also wore a helmet or captain's hat, which also made him an object of some derision. If you gave him the chance, he would corner you with a harangue.

When Greg Templeton bought the red Mercury convertible, for example, Ed scoffed.

"Convertible," he snorted. "What the fuck do you need a convertible for?" He gestured to his scooter. "I've always got a convertible."

As the story had it, Fred West defeated Ed in a race with a three-speed bicycle. But I didn't see that contest. I'm not sure where Ed worked but I don't think it was one of the car factories, where you could make good money. Riding a scooter, or anything on two wheels, was not a wise option in winter, so I don't know how he got around when the snow fell. The area is also the world capital of freezing rain. Nobody on two wheels will get far in that.

Another red convertible, a 1961 Ford with chrome rims, belonged to Danny Langlois, who lived on Grand Marais, not far from that big place that had the circular driveway. Danny was on the tall side, what was sometimes called "lanky," and had this great trick of driving from the passenger's seat so with the top down it looked like the car had no driver at all. He would tool past the A&W on Dougall that way, hoping someone would notice. Sometimes they did. Neither the Windsor police nor the OPP, the Ontario Provincial Police, ever seemed to be around when he pulled this trick. They would have bagged him for reckless driving. That is why car insurance was more expensive before age 25.

Danny viewed the convertible, purchased for him, I believe, by his father, as his key to success with the ladies. He found out that no vehicle could guarantee that. He was a handsome fellow but had these small ears that stuck out, which got him tagged "Oreos."

Mark Lantz said he was riding with Danny on Riverside Drive, when they saw this good-looking girl.

"Watch this," said Danny, who pulled up beside her.

"Hey baby, you wanna go for a ride?"

The girl turned and looked Danny over.

"Get fucked you ugly asshole," she said.

This method of "picking up girls," was quite common, and often worked. You then went "joyriding," with the possibility of submarine races. But not that day.

Larry Howe used to work at the A&W as a security guard, a "rent-a-cop," as we called them. Motorcycles were banned in there and he would chase them out. But even with Larry around mischief was the rule. I remember Dave Drayton hailing a carhop by saying, "Excuse me, slob?" I liked the A&W root beer, served in these cool glass mugs with big handles, but wasn't big on their food, dished up as Momma Burgers, Poppa Burgers, and Teen Burgers.

The Capri Pizzeria was next to A&W, and their parking lot was the preferred place to watch the traffic at the drive-in joint. Jim Dougall, who worked for Leo Ferri at his Shell station next door, used to eat there. Tony, the proprietor, nicknamed him "Gasoline."

"Gasoline good mechanic," he would say.

Jimmy, who was a good mechanic, could put away pizza like nobody. He would pile two and three pieces together and wolf them down like sandwiches.

I was in Capri one night when some older guy, who may have been a drunk, was very impatient to get his pizza, and angry at Tony.

"Come on Giuseppe, *get on with it!*" he said. The pizza there was good. Best in town, we would argue, and I can say I have never found better pizza anywhere. Their smallest size was a "baby," about the size of a pie plate. One night Tony asked someone what they wanted on their pizza. "Everything," he said, but then changed his mind. "Wait. No anchoozies." This story made the rounds.

Take a Dive

Windsor's humid summers can be brutal but our neighborhood had no public pool until about 1960, when Central Pool, in Central Park, finally came on line. So many kids were eager to get wet that they had to run the pool in shifts. The bicycle racks were off to one side and usually full. You had to pay, but I don't think it was more than a dime, or maybe a quarter. When waiting you could hang around the store off to one side, in a kind of annex, or do all the other stuff we used to do in the park.

Barb Bouffort, a rather robust girl who lived on McKay, worked in the store when not on duty as a lifeguard. Her older brother Paul was the athlete of the family and one of the fastest runners around, along with the Cushman brothers and a guy named Pat Hurley, whose bike showcased a warehouse of reflectors, emblems, mirrors, mudflaps and streamers. I remember watching Paul in a Massey football practice after school. He was wide open for a pass but the quarterback didn't see him.

"I was wide open, wop-eyes," Paul told him.

It was the first time I had heard this particular insult. Italians could also be called "grape stompers," because they made their own wine.

The Central Pool store sold the usual assortment of soft drinks, chips, popsicles and that stringy red licorice. One hot day Rick Michalski picked up a piece of dog shit, which might have been fake, and put it on the counter when Barb's back was turned. When she faced him and asked what he wanted, a stone-faced Rick pointed to the turd and said, "Got any of those in vanilla?"

That fit Rick's style of improvisational comedy. He could transform just about any situation into a skit. Years later he showed that ability in a donut shop where a hefty guy worked the counter. As Rick passed a patron pondering his selection he said "give us a coupla glazed, will ya fatso," and quickly retreated, leaving the patron to face the music.

The changing facilities inside the pool were always cramped and they had these wire baskets for your clothes and gave you a token in return. Towel flicking was a fine art somebody always aimed to redden your ass. I recall Pete Jones yelling at Michalski for this and Rick responding that he wasn't going to take any shit from any Pete Jones. Showering before going in the pool was required but you could sometimes slip through.

The pool itself was far too small and the lifeguards had their hands full, and would toss you for any nonsense. They were always telling everybody "no running on deck, no running on deck," as though you were on a ship. Industrial-strength levels of chlorine did not always prevent infected eyes and other complaints.

I can't remember anyone who couldn't swim but diving was something else. None of us had much of a clue what to do. A few, Lyle Goulet for instance, could perform a decent flip, even a one-and-a-half. Wayne Goulet was adept at these, which I could never pull off. Most of us could manage a jack-knife but we were more into causing a splash.

The best dive for this, if you did it right, was the can-opener, off the high board. You got as much lift as possible and went in feet first, holding one knee up to your chest with both hands and entering at a bit of an angle. Some guys would place their dive toward the tower, in an attempt to douse the lifeguards. The cannonball was another big splash. You would spring high and spread eagle as though about to belly-flop, then at the last instant tuck yourself into a ball. I also saw people perform the toe touch of the jack-knife, but then intentionally fail to straighten out, entering the water in a kind of inverted V that made a loud noise but not much splash. Others entered the water in a sitting position, which also made this great sound, though I don't think that one had a name.

Mark Lantz had this great "Jake the Snake" dive, sort of a spastic thing that always got a laugh. Two of the best divers were brothers, last name Tremblay. Russ Pollard also showed good form. Don Torchin hung around the pool a lot, but I can't remember him in the water. Maybe he was lusting in his heart after red convertibles. He could have pulled off a mean cannonball. But the biggest splash didn't go to the biggest guy, or girl. Technique had a lot to do with it, particularly on the can-opener. Some skinny guys could really bust them good. But I somehow doubt that anyone from the neighborhood went on to Olympic glory in diving.

I used to dive off the side and swim as far as I could underwater, nearly the whole length of the pool. And sometimes we would race from side to side. You'd be having a great time, then lifeguards Danny Metcalf or Jamie Beardmore would blow the whistle, and out you would go in a hurry with others filing in. We all had non-stop energy, but after these sessions I would usually go home. One day I said something to Beardmore about a dive he had just pulled off. He came outside and shoved me into the chain-link fence, which really hurt. We were thinking of getting Roger Goulet to go after

Beardmore but it never happened. It is also possible that Jamie would have kicked Roger's ass.

Another guy always around the pool was Ron Bates, this stringy blond kid, who looked something like Bob Jones. The protocol in those days, at least in school, was to refer to someone as Master, so Ron became Master Bates. He didn't think it was very funny. Wayne Pearce was another regular around the pool. Nobody seemed to like him and Dwayne Pickle once slapped him around. His sister Nancy used to go out with Bob Cushman.

The only alternative pool, in the official sense, was out at Beaver motel at Highway 3 and Walker Road, by the Windsor Drive-In. They had a diving board about twice as high as Central's, which was fun, but they maintained strict rules. No cut-off jeans allowed. It was a long bike ride, along busy roads, and I only went once or twice. They also charged more and their changing rooms were on the shabby side. In fact, they stunk.

Get Back, He's Cool

Curry Park was the local center for mumblypeg, a game played on the picnic table under the rain shelter. You took a jackknife, opened it to 90 degrees, stuck the tip in the table, put your finger other side of the blade as a kind of fulcrum, then flipped the other end. I can't detail the points system but if it stuck in with the handle up high, you measured how many fingers fit underneath. Having both ends touching the table was also good, and better still to have the knife jutting over the end of the table, which was pretty mangled from this game.

Out in the park kids also played "stretch," in which they stood face to face then threw an open jackknife. If it stuck in, the other kid would have to stretch out to that point. If he couldn't do it, he lost.

You could get up on the roof of the rain shelter pretty easy but getting down was a trick. I remember Ray Langlois trying to slide off and catching the ass of his pants on a nail. He hung there momentarily then fell and broke both his arms.

Central Park, much bigger, had a full football field which hosted AKO (Alpha Kai Omega) league games. Tom Hannan played in these as a pass receiver, and so did Jeff Mandel, a defensive lineman. Dave Fluke, another Glenwood student, was one of the better blockers. For its part, Curry Park hosted some great pickup football games among the older kids, which I used to watch. Dave Tregaskiss could punt the ball with a tight spiral, something I could never manage. His kicks went a long way. Brian Morency, built like a lineman, was another of the Curry gridiron players. There was a lot of talking before the ball was snapped, and I remember Brian warning that another reverse was coming. As I recall, these games were sometimes tackle.

I doubt he was much of a fighter but Brian's size could be intimidating. He was once at the A&W when some non-locals showed up in the mood for trouble. When this one guy started spouting off, Brian said, in mock terror. "Get back! Everybody back! He's cool!"

Brian's younger brother Wayne had some problem with his throat and spoke in an airy sort of high-pitched whine. He was always around Curry Park, which had the reputation as a place where bad language, dirty jokes and so on could be heard. This was true. Some of these jokes are the same heard across North America, spread by some kind of mysterious Internet. But the first time you hear them they are hilarious, shocking, or both. Some of these stories were vaguely theological.

There was the story of God putting some guy through all these tests, if you love me you will do such and such. God makes the guy hang off a cliff then knocks him off. On the way down, the guy asks why God did this. "Because you piss me off," God says.

As another had it, a kid is told that God is everywhere, then requests that God get out of his wagon, so he can pull it up the hill. And what stretches farther, skin or rubber?

"Skin, because Moses tied his ass to a tree and walked 40 miles."

To the melody of the old tune "Wake the Town and Tell the People," Mark Lantz would sing "bomb the town and kill the people." And to "You've Got to Have Heart," I heard "You've got to have a hard-on."

Sometimes the approach was more casual, while still scatological. "Why is shit tapered?" someone would calmly ask. "Because buns can't slam tight." This poem also made the rounds:

> She was goin' around the mountain at 90
> The chain on the motorcycle broke
> She landed in the grass, with a sprocket up her ass
> And her tits were playing ping-pong in the spokes.

Nobody seemed to know where these came from, or have any sense of authorship. Kids could respond to any statement with "Twat did you say? I beg your hard-on." And in certain situations, "you know, I cunt finger you out." People would ask "getting much?" someone would respond, "Off hand? Or on the hole?"

If something was particularly lame someone would say, "that's about as funny as a truck full of dead babies in front of an orphanage on mothers day." Others strove for the absurd. If a boat with two wheels rolls up on your lawn, how many pancakes does it take to cover a doghouse? Five, because ice cream doesn't have holes in it. That would be more of a groaner.

The word "fuck," of course, got a great workout as an all-purpose intensifier, but you didn't use it much, if at all, in mixed company. If you did, someone might say "nice talk," in a censorious kind of way. Very few girls used the term in those days and some kids would say, "make like the birds and *flock off.*"

When someone got really angry, with a showdown looming, the favorite phrase was "just fuck RIGHT off," as though the standard formulation of "fuck off!" yelled at the top of one's lungs, and accompanied by a jabbing finger, lacked the full capacity to convey a message of dislike.

Insult trends came and went, like clothing styles. For a time, people would tell someone to "just get down and puff on my ass."

People would also tell you to "pound salt," an abbreviation of "go pound salt up your ass with a two-by-four." I also heard members of the older generation using variations of this phrase, along with lines such as "okay, okay, don't get your shit in a knot," and, "You're just like a seagull. All you do is squawk and shit." And at a party at our house, Dr. Munholland was well into his cups and I heard him explain that Smokey the Bear's motto was "piss on it."

In those days you could also use the famous gesture of half a peace sign. Or you could jerk your extended thumb upward, a move sometimes accompanied by the phrase "sit on it and rotate." Another common phrase was "if you don't like it, you can lump it," though precisely what "lump it," meant I never learned.

"Little Miss Muffet, sat on her tuffet, eating her curds and whey, along came a spider and sat down beside her and said "hey, what's in the bowl, bitch?"

I heard this sometime in the fifth grade, at which level it belonged. Some decades later I heard it from a fifteenth-rate comic named Andrew Dice Clay. And then there was this: "Mary Mary quite contrary, how does your garden grow? Six little tulips, all in a row, and one fucking rabbit."

I don't remember who told it to me, probably Mark Lantz but it seemed funny at the time. A lot of it was in the telling, and some jokes would be meaningless to those not of our generation. For example, this black guy tells his girlfriend that Kodachrome is another name for Kotex. She duly ducks into a camera store to stock up but winds up attacking the clerk.

"I asked this man for Kodachrome," she explains, "and he asked me what size my Brownie was."

The famous Brownie camera has of course disappeared, along with the baking soda frogmen, hula hoops, and coonskin caps. The Davy Crockett hat was a hot item in Windsor when the series ran on Disney. I was photographed wearing one. It might have been a gift from my grandmother, who is in the picture.

There was a television commercial for Morton's pies, done by this Colonel Sanders type, whom Mark Lantz could imitate flawlessly. "Morton's Old Kentucky recipe pot pies," Mark would say, "Made by Li'l Abner, and the pot-pie people."

The Li'l Abner cartoon, by Al Capp, then a favorite, has long since disappeared.

Mark also called the odd color on one local car "pissbuckle brown" and he described some girl has having eyes like "two pissholes in a snow bank."

Sarcasm could get pretty thick. One day, I think in Curry Park, someone had dumped some piece of furniture, prompting some kid to say "what is this?"

"It's wood," someone said. "You know, the stuff they make trees out of."

While we were all middle-class kids of the post-war baby boom, and all pretty much alike, some sub-groups began to form. They weren't all-inclusive, of course, but "frats" and "greasers" were emerging. The frats wore these pants called "clamdiggers," made of light fabric, and which stopped at the calf. The frats favored light colors and striped t-shirts, and summer camps where they sang "Kum Bay Ya." They also liked songs by the Kingston Trio. The greasers were the "hard" guys with jeans, darker colors, who tended to smoke, aspired to drive a hot-rod, called people "pricks," and said things like "get down and puff on my ass." They preferred the more raucous rock and soul music, guys like James Brown. It was a version of the mods and rockers in Britain.

The Red Barn on Tecumseh Road was a frat kind of hangout. Dave Drayton once got in a fight there, as it was described to me, holding his arm out like a battering ram and running across the place until he scored impact.

I was in a car at the Red Barn once when bass player Ted Jablinski, probably not the correct spelling, came by. He was one of the first in town to have long hair and after he passed the car he whirled, stuck his head in the window and said, "did somebody in here make fun of me?"

Jack Girty, a guy known for thrift, would shut his engine off and coast into the Red Barn parking lot. If you went anywhere with Jack, he would make you pony up money for gas. Everybody did that but Jack was more stringent. He was also a stylish dresser and dancer.

Across from the Red Barn, the hot-rod set used this grocery store parking lot to show off their cars. Then they would make the circuit down to the Hi-Ho and back.

Not everyone fit in these camps of course. I didn't know Danny Napier very well because he went to Southwood school. He was crippled in one leg and walked with one crutch. A throat operation had left his voice scratchy, perhaps the reason for his nickname of "Scraper," and when he laughed, which was often, it sounded like a small outboard motor.

For all his limitations, Danny was a great snooker player. The girls liked him too, and he could charm them with wit and intelligence. He was actually a good-looking fellow, though on the small side, and he didn't let his misfortunes interfere with what we would call a normal life.

Like a Man in a Well

Like Detroit, Windsor was a big-time music town. Kerry Shapiro had his Nirvana band, and others included the Dukes of Windsor, Bobby Jay and the Nighthawks, the Middle Ages, and John Thomas and the Weepers. These and other groups would sometimes face off in a battle of the bands at Jackson Park, on Fireman's Field Day.

One group used to play on top of the concession stand at the Windsor Drive-in, while the patrons waited for it to get dark, so the submarine races could begin. The singer was about half a step flat and botched the words to Ray Charles' "Unchain My Heart." On the tune's bridge, for example, he would sing, "I'm under your spell, like a man in a well."

I wanted to play saxophone but there was a problem with that. This was not long after the big-band era, when saxophone players still doubled on clarinet. So the conventional wisdom, which was indeed wise, was that you first learned clarinet, a much more difficult and demanding instrument, then moved on to saxophone.

I duly learned "Don't Get Around Much Any More" and other tunes on the clarinet my uncle Steve gave me. The instrument was the older Albert system, which my teachers discouraged. I didn't know it at the time, but those old clarinets are valuable, and prized by dixieland players. I duly received a Bundy student model that surely wasn't up to the old one in tone quality. I took lessons from Terry Murphy, whose father, Phil Murphy, led the Caboto Club band, in which I played third clarinet, sitting beside Bob Buncick and in front of D'Arcy Templeton, Greg's younger brother, who played euphonium. D'Arcy was known for a droll sense of humor, and a certain sophistication. Like many other adults Mr. Murphy was often called "old man Murphy."

We played marches and rather pompous orchestral stuff like "Pacific Grandeur." My favorite piece was "Till There Was You," from *The Music Man* and later covered by the Beatles. Practices often got boring and Buncick and myself would sometimes play everything one note flat, but when we did this it was hard to contain laughter. Mr. Murphy was something of a purist and would sometimes ridicule the pop music of the day. I remember him making fun of "Bobby's Girl," a truly infantile ditty by Marcie Blaine that became a hit, at least locally. In front of the whole band, Mr. Murphy asked some woman at the Caboto Club if she wanted to be Bobby's girl. I don't recall the response but it was probably negative.

The Caboto Club was on Tecumseh Road, Windsor's "main drag," as adults would say. While we were waiting for a ride home some very strange people would come around, including some apparently itinerant girls scarcely older than me but looking very experienced. One pair was trying hard to impress Bob and myself. We were about to see what they had in mind when our ride showed up. The club itself was sometimes the site of massive United Auto Workers meetings. Band practice would be cancelled, but it was another reminder that what Chrysler builds builds Windsor, as the billboards proclaimed.

Bob and I used to listen to big-band recordings and anything on the charts with any sophistication, say "Harlem Nocturn," by the Viscounts, "Water Boy," by the Bill Shirley Trio, "Last Night" by the Mar-Keys, or the "Swingin' Shepherd Blues," by Mo Kaufman. But we didn't have access to enough good stuff, in any form, to keep us from being swept up in the tide of pop music, which in the late 50s could be pretty bad. Recall Sheb Wooley's "Purple People Eater," which, oddly enough, features jazzman Plas Johnson on saxophone. He's the tenor man on Henry Mancini's "Theme from the Pink Panther." King Curtis is the tenor player on many hits by the Coasters and I loved the saxophone solo by Gene "Big Daddy" Barge on the Chuck Willis version of "C.C. Rider." Barge is the "Daddy G" that Gary U.S. Bonds refers to in tunes such as "Quarter to Three."

Ricky Luckino, a trumpet player, took special lessons to master "Wonderland by Night," a ballad by Bert Kaempfert that somehow made the pop charts. Ricky hung around with Greg Morrell and his parents owned a couple of furniture stores, one on Howard.

We missed, unfortunately, most of the great jazz that was going on at that time. Consider 1959, when Coltrane recorded "Giant Steps," Paul Desmond wrote "Take Five," and Miles Davis released "Kind of Blue." It wasn't entirely our fault. Record companies inflicted rock on us, and we rolled with it.

Cubs and Scouts

For most of us, our parents loomed larger than life. Those who knew my father will recall his size 12 shoes, which I used to stare at with some amazement. Big shoes to fill indeed. In standoffs on the school playground there was sometimes a cry of "my dad can beat up your dad." But most of our dads had done all the beating up they were going to do. "What did your dad do in the war?" was a common query. They actually did quite a lot.

Deprived of their childhood by the Depression, they spent their late teens mixing it up with the Nazis. They got their reward, peace, and a free country, along with some monuments, including the Lancaster bomber that still stands in Jackson Park. The cenotaph memorializing "Our Glorious Dead," and Dieppe Gardens, recall an earlier conflict, which some I knew in Windsor, already in their emeritus years, referred to as the Great War.

Some of us joined the Air and Sea cadets, hanging out at HMCS Hunter on Ouellette Avenue. Alan McKenzie, my Glenwood friend, joined the Air Cadets and I remember him scoffing that the Sea Cadets only got to ride in a boat, whereas they went up in an actual airplane, though they were not yet ready to parachute. Aside from this our upbringing was about as non-military as one can imagine. For me anyway, some adult military types were uptight people to be avoided.

Once after school I was watching a football game at the adjoining field of Massey Collegiate. They had some ceremony that included the national anthem but at the time I was engaged in some play with other students, and not paying attention. Some guy in a military uniform, with a British accent and a pencil-thin mustache, sort of like Peter Sellers as Commander Lionel Mandrake in *Dr. Strangelove*, came over and ripped me pretty good. I explained to him that I went to Glenwood, not Massey, and that I was sort of off duty at the moment. He let me go, but he still looked as though, if it were in his power, he would have me thrown in the brig. I have no idea who he was and what he was doing there but my guess is he didn't see much action in the Big One.

Vincent Massey high school, initially Vincent Massey Collegiate Institute, was named after Canada's Governor General of the time, a man who did not figure largely in our thoughts. Before it was built they bussed us to a school in central Windsor for shop classes. The shop teacher was Mr. Philpott, a rather slovenly little man with thick glasses, bad teeth and a Napoleon complex. He gave me the strap one day for touching Stuart Galloway with a piece of wood that was still hot from the sander. I deserved it.

After Massey was completed we went to shop class there, with Mr. Aloysius Bellaire, a more genial instructor who could be easily distracted by getting him to talk about the war. One could easily believe that he had been present at every battle, land or sea. Mr. Bellaire was a genius on the lathe, and much concerned about safety. I made a rifle stock out of wood, a pretty useless project, but I did learn the basics of machinery. The shop had large windows and attracted many flies, which we used to pick off with rubber bands.

I later heard how some Massey students had got in trouble by making fake quarters, which they would cash in at the change machines at the small arcade within Woolco. They supposedly had a whole production line going and the case even attracted the RCMP since it dealt with counterfeiting.

All told, not much distinguished us from kids in Michigan, but in some ways the British tradition was still strong then. We opened our classes at Glenwood Public School with "God Save the Queen," not "O Canada." Likewise the Cub Scouts, in which I did participate, at the Paulin Memorial Presbyterian Church, are of British derivation, founded by Lord Baden-Powell. But this organization, for all its quirks, was hardly military.

While we carried on in the church basement, kids who weren't scouts looked in the windows. I suppose it was a kind of spectacle, moving around in a circle on your haunches, chanting "we are the cubs of the red six," etc. Actually I used to swing by the proceedings of Canadian Girls in Training (CGIT) at Glenwood United Church on Grand Marais, though it wasn't clear what, exactly, they were training for. Wendy Walmsley, who went to Northwood, was a CGIT member, and I was fond of her. She would show up at local dances. Another early flame was Michelle Pilon, who went to Cahill and lived on the other side of Huron Line. Dave Renn, known as a "hard" guy, also had his eye on Michelle.

One night I was hanging around the CGIT crowd and for some reason David Andrews showed up. He was a fellow student at Glenwood and had been born in China of missionary parents. I think they bailed after Chairman Mao's gang took over, a wise move. Anyway, in this house next to the church, the upstairs bedroom was open, and we saw this woman, about 30 I would guess, disrobing at a leisurely pace. It seemed she was checking out her own equipment in a mirror, even as we checked it out too. Maybe it is true that the best things in life are free.

Seeing women naked purely by chance was a rare thing but you could do so in a more formal sense. Detroit was also home to the Empress Burlesque, right down by the waterfront, and which virtually every Windsor kid visited. They would let anybody in if they had money. The place featured a stage show, with chorus lines. Then one of the star dancers would come out, solo, and audition her gear for the audience. Sometimes an announcer would break in and say "start making some noise or she won't go all the way."

Glenwood United, meanwhile, was down the road from an abandoned place that became known as the "haunted house." How it had come to be that way nobody seemed to know. The place had this awful musty smell, but we would poke around there anyway. It was indeed kind of spooky and I never ventured in at night. Every neighborhood should have a haunted house. This one eventually burned down, I believe, probably arson or just kids playing with matches.

I earned a few Cub scout badges, and got into the Mowgli lore and all that. I passed the semaphore phase and got credit for starting a garden but had a lot of trouble with the knots, anything past a simple clove hitch. My attempts at the more complicated knots baffled my instructor, one of the Bradshaws. My father knew all these knots, from bowline to sheepshank. So did John Tregaskiss, who like his brother Dave attained the rank of queen scout, quite an accomplishment, kind of like being in the special forces, and duly announced in the *Sandwich West Herald*.

The scouting regime included a weekend at Camp Henry on the east side of Point Pelee. The water was absolutely freezing and the beach more gravel than sand. The facilities weren't exactly luxurious. In the scouting lexicon, the latrine was a "caibo," pronounced as in Maracaibo, a city in Venezuela.

During this weekend, Alan Gordon drew a reprimand for using foul language. Alan lived near Dougall and you would see him everywhere. He always seemed to materialize when you were in the woods, particularly Devonshire Bush. Alan was a year or two older and, like Colin Middleton, prided himself on being knowledgeable about sex. He was also kind of a tough guy, though I never saw him mix it up. His brother Donald was my age, and more of what we would call a "nice guy." My mother had taught both of them and knew their parents, who went to our church.

At this camp I heard a version of "Moonlight Bay," with this refrain:

The worms crawl in, the worms crawl out
They go in thin, they come out stout
Your eyes fall in, your guts decay
And that's the end of a wonderful day

This period was of course the height – or depths – of the Cold War, but we did not hide under our desks in nuclear drills as did our contemporaries across the border. We were aware of communism and the Soviet Union, but all that seemed so far away. This was the post-war world of peace and prosperity, which we could see all around us. The road ahead seemed to lead only to limitless distance, though not many of us had figured out what we were going to do. Life was good, life was without want, and life was fun. Yes, above all else, it was about fun. Everything was an opportunity for a punch line. The time when the door opens and lets the future in would come later, and in strange ways.

This is My Father's World

I would guess that the hood was about 50-50 Catholic and Protestant, and churches abounded, but religion was something we seldom discussed. I never heard of anyone being shunned or excluded because of religion. However, one male substitute teacher, whose name now escapes me, asked me where I went to church and I told him our family went to a Presbyterian church. "That's the worst of the bunch," he said, without explanation, a remark that bothered me for some time, though I didn't say anything to my parents.

John Fox, the minister at Paulin Memorial, was the father of Bob Fox, who went to Central School. We knew each other from Sunday school, more a kind of babysitting than a form of serious religious instruction. They would pass out these sort of comic books of "Adventures in Bible Times" with some character named Tullus.

One of the hymns went "hark, hark, hark, while infant voices sing," which we would change to "fart, fart, fart, while infant voices sing."

The hymn I liked best was "This Is My Father's World," which suited children's voices. Even now it can make me look up. So could the Rev. Fox.

His shiny bald head made him seem to glow. You could tell he was serious, a man of prayer and true spirituality. I can say without reservation that he was a godly man. Later in the 1960s, Bob and I, hair down past our shoulders, took it upon ourselves to tell him he was all wrong, that he needed to read Paramahansa Yogananda and, in effect, go east old man. And drugs were cool too. The Rev. Fox listened carefully, but must have been wondering where his early preaching went wrong.

This substitute teacher, bald and middle-aged, who put down my church, was a big partisan of student Lisa La Croix, one of the few Catholic students at Glenwood. He evidently thought that at a so-called "Protestant," school, Lisa would be the target of anti-Catholic abuse, which never happened. The girl who took more abuse than anyone was Margaret Wallace, who was English, with a strong accent, and on the snootie side to boot. She was also rather odd looking, with a flat face and hair that always looked dirty. If she touched something kids would say "Wallace cooties. Wallace cooties."

Corrine Musgrave, a very nice girl from a rather pious Baptist home, for some reason got tagged "Draino." Another girl, on the large side, was labeled "Gorgo." She had thick eyebrows and what would now be called "big hair."

I thought Catholics in general were more devout but was disturbed by a copy of *My Little Missal*, a Catholic instructional text I found in our front yard. It showed a rather overheated fate for those unlucky enough to be outside the fold of the Catholic Church. I asked my mother about this and in her ecumenical way she assured me that we were all God's children. That made sense to me.

Politics, likewise, rarely intruded into our discussions. Nobody identified anybody as Liberal, Conservative, CCF, or whatever. I consider this a good thing. Adults of course argued politics but most kids found it boring. John Diefenbaker, Canadian Prime Minister, was not exactly charismatic, and neither was Dwight Eisenhower. John Kennedy was a dashing star by contrast.

The Catholics had these great stories about nuns and priests. At St. Gabriel's the prevailing heavy was brother Aquinas, who wore lumberjack boots and was known to kick over a desk in the course of a tirade. The nuns were fond of rapping knuckles with a ruler, like the "penguin" in *The Blues Brothers*. Judging by what happened when everybody got to high school, there wasn't a whole lot of difference in the quality of education. At Glenwood they worked us hard, but we were better off for it.

Only the Catholic girls wore official school uniforms. You could say that the rest of us wore unofficial uniforms. Under the principle of centershot, wearing the right clothing was of the utmost importance. The store of choice for guys was Brotherhood, down on Ottawa St., where they had this huge pair of Levis up on the wall. You could occasionally find items that fit the bill at Sentry or Woolco, but the good stuff required a trip to Detroit, whose stores and styles were more up to date. The Canadian dollar was also worth more at the time, a reality that hurt my father, who lived in Canada and worked in Detroit.

We would save money from allowance, paper routes, collecting bottles or whatever then prowl through vast downtown department stores such as Hudson's, which every year brought out this huge American flag. You would buy pants and wear them underneath an older pair, hoping the customs guy wouldn't notice. If any did, they said nothing. With shoes you wore an old pair and left them at Flagg Bros. or Tom McCann. And you would sometimes try to dirty up the new pair so the customs guy wouldn't notice. Anything we bought was probably well within the limit so this was all a waste of time and effort. But there was one style of shoe we all wanted.

They were a kind of cross between slippers and moccasins, in a dark reddish-brown leather, with black highlights over the stitching. The soles were very small and part of the leather upper touched the ground. They wore through easily and I remember the snow getting into mine, a soaker as it were. But these shoes were very cool, the vanguard of hip, and you just had to have them. In those shoes, you would never be centered out.

I displayed mine proudly one day at Rak 'n Snak, when this guy from another part of Windsor showed up to challenge the locals at snooker. He was admiring my shoes and asked me where I got them. He said he usually played pool at Red's Recreation, which he called Red's Wreck.

The Beatle-type shoes, with the elastic and that loop at the back to help put them on, were also popular. They had what we called "Cuban heels," and you put metal cleats on them. Teachers hated the noise they made. It was still pretty common to have shoes resoled and the local shoemakers, usually somewhat gruff foreign guys, were always busy.

Running shoes remained in style for sports and casual situations, and were heavily advertised, as in this ditty for U.S. Kedds.

If you want shoes with lots of pep,
Get Kedds, kids, Kedds.
For bounce and zoom in every step,
Get Kedds, kids, Kedds.
You'll be a champion with style, you'll hit that ball a half a mile.
They're tough, they last a long, long while.
Kedds, kids, Kedds.

Red Ball Jets were an alternate brand of sneaker, not as popular and sometimes mocked as "Green Ball Bombers."

Some of our attempts at humor were based on products and television commercials. "Hear what happened to Helene Curtis?" someone would say. "Max Factor," came the answer. In a variation of this one, Betty Crocker burned her buns. There was also this: What is black and runs through rice fields? Answer: Uncle Ben. And the strongest substance in the world? Ex-Lax, because it can knock the shit out of Superman.

Lame attempts could bring the deadpan response of "wasn't funny." And for a time, people would respond to a groaner by saying "who are you talking to?"

Another occasionally funny kid lived in the red brick one-story next to Christ the King school. Wayne Rennie, who I met through Mark Lantz, played baseball and every summer would ask a friend to spend a week at their cottage "up north," as we would say. In Canada, we were as far south as you can go. I never made the trip but I did hang out with Wayne from time to time. One day he was running around the house singing, "come take a peek through my peek-a-boo kaleidoscope," the only line in the song. I remember Wayne pointing to spot just above his solar plexis and proudly saying "I'm double-jointed here." Wayne wasn't big but he was a pretty good fighter.

He looked a bit like a guy I will call Bernie Muntz, someone I really hated, who would sneak up behind you and cram your face full of snow. We called this trick a "face wash," but it wasn't much fun for the one on the receiving end. Years later I was very glad to hear that John Tregaskiss had cleaned Muntz's clock. It was like being cut off by a speeding driver, only to see the offender pulled over by a cop farther down the road.

He Shoots He Scores

With hockey forbidden at Glenwood you sometimes played in the frozen streets. When they dug the excavation for the Massey gym it filled with water then froze. On Christmas, 1959, I received a Montreal Canadiens jersey. I put it on and took my skates down to the Massey rink, where other kids had also gathered. I lost my puck that day, so we played with a rock. The ice was soft, but no one fell through. When the thaw came kids were out with rafts before the construction crew could finish the job. I remember seeing Tom Hannan out there on a raft, kind of a Mark Twain scene.

My dad would sometimes drive us to River Canard, where I caught my first fish, a black bass. I remember it because that day I also dragged up a fishing rod. I cleaned it up and used it, another early example of recycling. In winter River Canard was a great spot for skating. We would go near the concrete bridge by St. Joseph's church, where kids organized pick-up hockey games. Some guys would provide their own commentary, like the announcers on "Hockey Night in Canada."

"It's Frank Mahovlich, winding up in his own end. Mahovlich works his way to center, around the defense. . . *He shoots he scores!*"

And so on. Bill Hewitt, son of Foster Hewitt, was the play-by-play man at the time. *The Hockey Night In Canada* staffers like Ward Cornell were national figures. So was Murray Westgate, the ESSO man. "The ESSO sign of confidence, the happy motoring sign," their slogan said. They also construed ESSO as Esso Sure Safe Oil Heat.

You could also listen on radio, when games were not on television. King Clancy, a former player, was one of the regulars on the "Hot Stove League," feature between periods.

Like many others I "skated on my ankles," which nobody can do. The phrase means that my skates fit poorly, and were poorly tied. But I joined in some of the games. To play organized hockey was a much more complicated undertaking than baseball, and required more commitment, both time and money, than some parents were willing to make. The Koellin brothers, Pat and Mike, played hockey and so did Ken Havens, who also refereed. The Koellins, both red-haired and heavily freckled, had some contact with the Detroit Red

Wings and would show up with goalie sticks that had been owned by Terry Sawchuk, one of the all-time greats.

If you just wanted to skate you could go to the Windsor Arena on certain days. But there was a problem. You had to keep moving. If you stopped and grabbed the boards, an arena employee would try and rap your hands with a stick. And some of the older skaters would body-check smaller kids to the ice.

Few Canadians made it to baseball's major leagues or the National Football League but at that time more than 90 percent of the players in the National Hockey League were Canadians. While the Detroit Tigers were the team of choice for Windsorites in baseball, Toronto and Montreal vied for the hockey loyalties. I was a Montreal fan and Jean Beliveau was my favorite player. I had one of those hockey calendars, with the Canadiens team of 1957-8, with players like Jean-Guy Gendron, Doug Harvey, Jean-Guy Talbot, Bernie "Boom Boom" Geoffrion, Tom Johnson, Jacques Plante and Bert Olmstead, who looked a lot like my father. The breakfast cereal boxes of the time had hockey tips from NHL players. I remember one by Maurice "Rocket" Richard, the Canadiens star, showing the proper way to perform the poke check.

Richard was reported to have the fastest backhand shot, some 85 mph. The fastest slap shot clearly belonged to Bobby Hull of the Chicago Blackhawks, the "Golden Jet." They allowed more radically curved sticks then and Hull's slapshot could hit 120 mph, about 20 mph faster than the hardest shooters now. My sense is that Hull, a kind of Jim Brown on skates, could have shot the puck that fast with any stick. Goalies said that Hull was going to kill someone and it was about this time that the Canadiens' Jacques Plante started wearing a mask, the first NHL goalie to do so. We discussed the merits of the mask briefly in class at Glenwood.

Some Windsorites were fans of the Red Wings but the ongoing debate concerned who was better, Maurice Richard or Gordie Howe, an absolute deity in Detroit. A record on AM radio proclaimed, "Gordie Howe is the Greatest of Them All." The Red Wings' announcer, Bud Lynch, decked out Howe's every move in breathless commentary, and you thought the Wings were the only team on the ice.

The local squad, the Windsor Bulldogs, then part of the Ontario senior league, featured Lou Bendo and Irwin Gross, with Wayne Rutledge in goal. They vied for the Allan Cup. I went to their game with the Galt Terriers and one leather-lung behind the bench kept calling the Galt players "tarpapers." I still don't understand the insult. Goulet was with me that day and somebody threw a battery on the ice. The Bulldogs played in the Windsor Arena, a cramped barn of a place with hopelessly small seats.

A lot of hockey was played on those table-top games with the spinning players controlled by rods. I first played these at the home of Gary Barker, on Dominion. It was an older model and the players did not slide back and forth, only rotated, except the goalie, who could be moved back and forth across the goalmouth We played with a marble for a puck. Gary had a set of names for the players, Getaway Peewee and so on. Nobody held much of an edge. We would offer commentary along the Hockey Night In Canada style as we played. For Christmas one year my parents bought a hockey game with sliding players. My brother Phil and I played many a game but I still liked Gary's old set. Without the sliding players, you could control the puck and take time to set up your shot. With sliding players things got rowdy.

Gary also introduced me to professional basketball. His favorite team was the St. Louis Hawks and his favorite player Bob Pettit. A few games were on television and I recall players like Clyde Lovellette, Bill Russell, and Sam and K.C. Jones. There was also a seven-footer named Walt Dukes who was pretty awkward, as my father once commented. When Wilt Chamberlain came along, he dominated, but the Boston Celtics were the best team.

In Windsor every year they announced the "all city" selections in major sports. They would give obvious data, informing the reader that Mario Baggio, for example, was of "Italian descent." When Wayne Morgan got the nod, maybe from Patterson high, it was "Negro descent." Wayne got a scholarship to Simon Fraser University, the only such deal I can recall. I don't know if the all-city football players such as Ed Potomski or Ray Trudelle made the grade in college.

One occasionally heard the canard that blacks did not opt for hockey because they had "weak ankles." That would have surprised Willie O'Ree, first black player in the National Hockey League. As it happened, Ferguson Jenkins, the standout pitcher for the Chicago Cubs and other teams, was from nearby Chatham and a terrific hockey player, better than he was at baseball in the early going. Nobody charged that those of Japanese descent had weak ankles. The Wakabayashi brothers, Herb and Mel, played for the Chatham Maroons and were always getting headlines in the sports section of the *Windsor Star*.

The *Star* also covered the hydroplane races on the Detroit River, near Belle Isle, also a big deal for the three Detroit dailies, the *Detroit Times*, *Detroit Free Press*, and *Detroit News*, all with some readership in Windsor. People lined the waterfront on both sides to watch and I suspect crashes were the attraction for many, as they are in auto racing. Those things were incredibly loud and kicked up a huge rooster tail. I can't recall the names of the drivers but I believe Miss Supertest, a Canadian entry, won in 1959. Other big names included Miss Detroit, Miss Bardahl and Miss Budweiser.

Though it wasn't really a sport, professional wrestling also enjoyed quite a following.

The master of ceremonies was Lord Layton, a hulking man purporting to be a Brit, a former champion wrestler who sometimes threatened to go back into the ring to teach some upstart a lesson. The prevailing stars of the time were Dick the Bruiser, Bobo Brazil, Killer Kowalski, Leapin' Larry Chene, the Sheik, and such brawlers as Hardboil Hagerty. Killer Kowalski was supposedly a "scientific" wrestler who had perfected a paralyzing claw hold. Bobo Brazil was famous for his head-butt. Some were absolute freaks, like Haystack Calhoun, who weighed in around 600 pounds, and Happy Humphrey, who topped 700. The back of their necks looked like stairs.

Dick the Bruiser, a former football player with the Green Bay Packers, was always a villain, and they would throw him in with some kid, a new golden boy, who would have his way for a while before the Bruiser humiliated him. The Bruiser once turned a fire extinguisher on a downed wrestler. Years later Rick Michalski, known as Rags, used one of those to exit from the Riviera, a bar on Dougall, holding it on his back and blasting out like Rocket Man. I think that might have been the time he was ejected for playing a kazoo.

Everybody knew the wrestling was "fake" and most of the wrestlers were sacks of flab, but we still watched and talked about it. I don't know what that says about us, but I'm not going to let it bother me. Bud Lantz, Mark's father, really got into it, and so did his mother, Eileen. My parents hated it. For them, it was another version of "The Three Stooges." But they had their own favorites.

In addition to "Cheyenne," my father liked "The Honeymooners." So we got to know Ralph, Alice, Norton and Trixie pretty well. I liked the "Robin Hood" series but seldom saw a whole episode because it conflicted with my paper route with Paul Bradshaw. The same thing happened with "The Buccaneers," but other kids would fill me in. In one episode this sailor named Gaff wound up with a knife in his back. It was likely these shows that prompted kids to get in these mock sword fights, using garbage can lids as shields. "Get stabbed," was something kids would say to each other.

My parents would not let me watch "Naked City," but I did see that show at Shepherd's across the street, where I sometimes babysat. It was tough stuff for the time but now part of the vast television slag heap. "There are eight million stories in the naked city. This has been one of them," the show said at the end. The theme music featured an evocative trumpet line. In the course of the program they would sometimes show a place called "Wang Chu's Laundry," which sparked some jokes.

Life's a Holiday

During the Christmas season I would have to say things got pretty materialistic. The conventional wisdom is that Depression Era parents did not want their children to be deprived, as they were, and so went overboard on the gift side. There is some truth to that but we responded with eager collaboration. You had this list of stuff you wanted and you paid close attention to what other kids got. The question of presents blurred the religious significance of the holiday. I remember singing this.

> We three kinds of orient are,
> Trying to smoke a loaded cigar
> It blew up and here we are
> Far away on yonder star.

One of the kids at my dad's archery club, Baron Christianson or Christensen, composed a variation on "Little Drummer Boy" that went "rup-a-pum-pum, smell my bum."

In Windsor and Detroit Christmas was more gray than white. Snow turned to slush that clung to cars like sucking eels. This made getting around dangerous, but you had a week of freedom to play with your new stuff. Then you would compare notes with the schoolmates you hadn't seen over the holiday. Nobody really wanted clothes for Christmas, but if you got them you usually wore them the first day – unless they centered you out. The items of choice were model cars, road-race sets, Meccano sets, record players, that kind of thing.

I wanted a BB gun. The Daisy company made them and owning one really set you apart. I had one briefly, which I used to shoot the bird through the milk chute. Before that I had a lever-action air rifle that did nothing but make a noise. You could, however, cram some dirt down the barrel. The air would pop out the clod about 10 feet at best.

Some kids had those single-shot pellet guns that fired .177 lead projectiles. These were dangerous, and so were the BB guns, which fired copper balls that could break glass. When you were prowling through Rankin Bush, or Bozo Bush, you would sometimes come across kids with these guns. I actually wanted a .22 rifle like the ones I saw in the sporting magazines my dad read.

It was not to be, but my dad did make bows and arrows for us, and took us shooting, both out in the country and at Riverside Recreation Center, which the Windsor Bowmen rented for competitions. Dad received awards for a "six gold," that is, six arrows in the bull's-eye. And he was the first club member to shoot a deer.

It took a few years but he got one, over in central Michigan. I remember walking to the corner of Grand Marais and Huron Line, down by the Sandhill House, and watching for his car. When he brought the deer home, local kids were looking in our windows.

"Hey kid," one said to me. "There's a reindeer in your basement."

My dad would also take me out of school on Memorial Day, an American holiday, and we would go ground-hog hunting up by Thamesville. You had to sneak up on these things, but he bagged a few. One of his friends picked them off at long range with a .222 rifle. I remember it had a light-colored stock and a long scope. The local farmers were happy to be rid of the pests, and the county even paid a bounty on them.

On the other hand, wildlife was not always a target.

One of my father's favorite spots was Jack Miner's bird sanctuary out by Kingsville, where the geese land by the thousands in their beautiful formations, sounding the trumpet as they touch down. Dad would drive the family out there after church on a Sunday afternoon. As locals and tourists can attest, it's quite a sight.

Halloween transformed the streets into a kind of bizarre mall. I wore a skeleton suit and dutifully covered many blocks, returning with a pillow case full of candy. Everybody was trying to outdo everybody else, and one got to know which houses handed out the good stuff and who were the tightwads. But the tightwads didn't experience much retaliation. Maybe someone would soap their windows, a rather common prank. There were the usual stories of apples rigged with razor blades and so on but I never knew any victims of such an attack. Apples were never a favorite unless they were "candy" apples. Candy bars were premium, along with that candy corn, toffee and such. I did know of older kids who stole candy from smaller trick-or-treaters. Overall the biggest winners were the dentists, and going to the dentist at that time was no fun.

Some houses would make you do something for your treat, sing a song or whatever, and would give extra for a good costume. Halloween also occasioned taunts such as: "why don't you just put peanut butter on your mouth and go out as an asshole?" and "pull a plastic bag over your head and go out as a prick." I never saw anyone take up either challenge.

Victoria Day, May 24, became simply "firecracker day," the late British queen not one to occupy a huge place in our affections. They sold just about everything in those days, from four-inch cannon crackers down to "Ladyfingers," the tiny outfits about an inch long and the width of a pencil lead. You lit one wick and about 50 of them went off at the pace of a Sten gun. Sparklers and all kinds of rockets were also available. The firecrackers all came in this thin red paper and the labels bore Chinese characters. Firecracker day sounded like full warfare and my parents hated it. We'd save some of these munitions for later use, but you didn't want to be caught bringing fireworks to school.

The biggest fireworks show came during the Freedom Festival celebrating July 1, Dominion Day (now Canada Day) and American Independence Day, July 4. Barges in the Detroit River launched the fireworks and thousands lined the waterfront on both sides. Those on Belle Isle (USA) and maybe Peche Island (Canada) got the best view, aside from those who happened to be on the Ambassador Bridge.

Probably the happiest day of the year, surpassing even Christmas, was the last day of school, June 29 or thereabouts. The final week you could feel the excitement building, and of course the last day nothing got accomplished. If you didn't know it by then, it was too late. You got your final report card and they let everyone out early.

On the way home, groups of kids, of all ages, would be belting out this masterpiece:

No more pencils, no more books
No more teachers' dirty looks
Drop your pencil in the well
Tell your teacher, go to hell

Sometimes we just repeated the first two lines. When I think of it now this poem evokes a response of delight. Two months of freedom and good times lay ahead, and those two months seemed like years. Never has the pace of life been so slow, and it was absolutely wonderful. With this seemingly endless stretch of sunny weather came the prospect of adventure. Central Park, Curry Park, Devonshire pond, Cowpaddy Lake, downtown Detroit, Bozo Bush, the railyards, Ashton's Motel, Rak n' Snack, the Dairy Bar. And much more. A song by Bobby Rydell, "Wildwood Days," said "Every day's a holiday, and every night is Saturday night." Summers were like that.

I remember the tune because my father took us to Wildwood Lodge, up on the Bruce Peninsula, where we caught sacks of perch and pickerel. You put them in the cooler, made a note of what you had caught, and they served you the fish for dinner. I made friends with the people who ran the place, who had kids my age. The other kids you met you never saw again. Dad also took us to Round Lake, in Algonquin Park, a more rustic setup. On the drive back he would sing some Merchant Marine ditties.

Just about all families made similar jaunts. These vacations sometimes affected your baseball league, or caused you to miss a party. But there was no getting out of it and you enjoyed it even if you didn't say so.

Most summer days I would get up early, jump on my bike and take off, first for Curry Park, then Central, then maybe Woolco or the Dairy Bar. You would run into some people, Johnny Maxwell, Lyle Goulet, whoever, and make plans from there. Central and Curry Parks were a kind of home base. You could do quite a lot in one day, and ride pretty far on your bike, sometimes even to LaSalle. But whatever you did, you always made it back for dinner. Then you would go out again.

One good summer day trip was Bob-Lo island, derived from the French *bois blanc*. Bob-Lo is a Canadian Island near the point where the Detroit River empties into Lake Erie, but an American company ran the island's amusement park. Getting there was an international experience. You would take the tunnel bus to Detroit and get on one of the two Bob-Lo boats down by the foot of Woodward. The Columbia and the St. Clair could each hold about 2000 people. These ships gave the feeling of an ocean cruise, but the trip took little time, just enough to get into mischief. I remember asking the band to play "Tequila," a hit for the Champs in 1958 and one of the last "instrumental" hits to feature the saxophone, like "Honky Tonk," by Bill Doggett, with the great Clifford Scott on tenor. That day the band declined to play "Tequila," and I don't remember what they played.

Car Culture

It made perfect sense that all of us had the time and means for amusement. Windsor and Detroit, after all, formed the epicenter of the auto industry, then booming, and with little foreign competition. Just about everyone in town was tied to the auto business in some way. The introduction of new models was a major event and Chrysler used to put this plastic on the fences in an attempt to avert prying eyes.

Harry Ouellette, Tom and Jim's father, was a sales manager at one of the Ford dealerships, maybe Dingwall. I remember when the first Toyotas hit town. The rather boxy little cars had Mr. Ouellette rolling with laughter. "Toy-toas" he called them. We all thought they were a joke. After all, this was the era of the muscle car.

I remember when Tony Marantette bought one of those Shelby Mustangs with the 428 engine and scoops all over it. It was a metallic blue and he would park it at Leo Ferri's Shell station on Dougall, where people would pull in just to look at the thing. Tony also drove an Austin Healey into which he had dropped a 283 Chevy V-8. That thing would really move. I recall that it had quiet mufflers, which made it what we called a "sleeper," but the Chevy engine required that the hood be raised a bit, kind of a giveaway.

To be the kind of person who could swap and modify engines and build a unique car was high status indeed. Many kids prized this kind of practical, engineering knowledge over what they learned in school. To be able to tinker with cars for a living, well that would be the perfect job.

The real master mechanic in the neighborhood was Barry Maskery, who lived near Dougall. I remember him as tall and athletic, with chiseled features, and totally immersed in cars, the perfect aptitude for Windsor at that time.

Not far away, behind Devonshire Bush, near the old Kenilworth track, someone had cleared a small race course for go-carts and mini-bikes. Barry had rigged a go-kart with some kind of screaming engine, maybe from a chain saw, that left everything else in the dust. There were also some go-kart tracks around Windsor, where you paid a dime a lap, but these were pretty tame. Barry moved on to work as a mechanic and to drive a muscle car. I remember he later had a Chevy II with the 350 engine, or maybe a 427, altered of course. At stoplights the thing would shake like a laundromat dryer, and you thought the engine would blow itself apart. But when it hit high revs, it made very sweet music.

A V-8 engine was absolutely *de rigueur*. All sixes were considered gutless and a four was a complete joke. Some allowance was made for sports cars, however. I remember when an MG pulled away from the Dairy Bar, and Jimmy Dugal and I counted as he shifted through the four gears. The ideal setup was a "V8 stick," though some automatics were acceptable. The ones in the Oldsmobiles had this gear marked S, for Super. Kids made jokes about how some guy thought that R meant "race" and L "long trips."

The racing celebrities often showed up at Detroit Dragway, which ran these wonderful radio ads "Sundaaaaay! Sunday at Detroit Dragway. Big Daddy Don Garlits versus Don 'the Snake,' Prudhomme," and so on. We snuck in a couple of times by scaling a fence. Except for the rail jobs, it wasn't that exciting, almost like standing beside a freeway, particularly with the stock cars. When a Jaguar XKE lost a race Danny Langlois said "The next guy who tells me those things are fast I'm going to punch him in the mouth."

The stock car races at Checkered Flag, on Highway 2, and Bluebird Raceway, on Howard, were actually more exciting. Stan Earish dueling with Johnny Banks and others in '32 Ford coupes, late 1940s sedans, even some Studebakers, all pretty battered. I think Hawkeswood Garage and Merrifield's Body Shop were among the sponsors, many of them car places. You watched the heats, the features, the Australian pursuit. This was authentic local stuff, with local heroes. I once rode out to Checkered Flag with Lyle and Roger Goulet. I was hoping Roger would drive fast on the way back, but he didn't.

Our idols included athletes, race drivers, and musicians from across the river. I remember John Tregaskiss, in the Glenwood school yard, singing "Show Me a Man Who's Got a Good Woman," by Joe Tex. Several groups had a go at "Shake a Tail Feather." Edwin Starr of "Agent Double-O Soul" was the epitome of style.

On Emancipation Day, American blacks – "Negroes" was the correct term then – would pour into Windsor's Jackson Park for barbecues, many riding full-dress Harley-Davidsons. They never had any trouble that I can recall. There were no Ku Kluckers in Windsor, not known as a center of bigotry. Some years later, however, when Lynn Gatrall began dating Ken Smith, who was black, some locals thought this was out of line. I need a witness here, but I think someone may have spray painted something not very nice about Ken on the Gatrall home, over on Roselawn Drive. Had Lynn's new boyfriend not been black, it's dubious that simple jealousy could have provoked such an act.

Some locals had drawn conclusions about blacks from the area in Detroit around John R and Brush, teeming with hookers, pimps and drunks. That was like judging white people by Windsor's "Tin Can Alley," a rather raggedy area between Third Concession and Tecumseh. And whenever anyone used the Brush St. area to attribute certain traits to all blacks, the Sheehan family always came up. They lived on Curry and their place was always a mess.

The dominant prejudice in the hood among younger people was not racial, economic, ethnic or religious but anti-rural. Anything smacking of rural life got plastered with ridicule. People from the country were "plowboys," and those from "up north" were "bush boys." It was this attitude that produced quips such as Mark Lantz's observation that such and such a person "fell out of hillbilly heaven, on his head," based on the Tex Ritter song. In the argot of the neighborhood, to be such a person was the ultimate centershot.

We made fun of Puce, French for "flea," a small town near Lake St. Clair. For us, people from Puce were hicks, and people would say things like "he has the fastest boots west of Puce." The place wasn't much different than a dozen small towns in Essex County. It was near Emeryville, a kind of party spot in summer, with a dance pavilion at the beach. It drew good crowds but one day when I showed up there was only this one fat guy playing tunes on the juke box, dancing around by himself, and staring out at the lake.

I got a challenge to my own anti-rural prejudices when my father took us up near Hanover to look at some property. The place bordered a lake and dad was seriously thinking of buying it and moving the family there, though it wasn't clear what kind of work a mechanical engineer could find in the area. The place was beautiful and I liked the idea at the time. But there was some legal question about the boundaries and the deal never happened. We would move on, however, in due course. As far as I was concerned, it came at the worst possible time, and to the worst possible place.

No More Pencils, No More Books

Dougall Avenue actually turns into Highway 401. In other words, one of the main streets of our life suddenly becomes the road out of town, leading to who knows where, maybe limitless distance, maybe not. Even in a prosperous town, where there was plenty of work, it was inevitable that some of us, maybe most, would leave. Not everyone wants to spend years assembling Dodge Monaco automobiles on three shifts, even with good pay and benefits. And after all, most of our parents had come here from somewhere else. Why should it be any different with us? In my case, the departure had nothing to do with me, and was strictly involuntary.

My father had grown up on a farm, in the wide open spaces of Saskatchewan, and aspired to own some property and build his own house. The brick bungalow at 3116 McKay was obviously inadequate, especially for someone his size, and with three growing boys. Phil and I had to share a room and we all had to share one bathroom. When I first grasped what a move would mean I tried to argue against it but when my dad made up his mind to do something there was no stopping him. The first step in getting what you want is knowing what it is, and he knew what he wanted.

He bought 40 acres in Colchester North township, about 15 miles away, at the end of the village of McGregor, on Middle Side Road. This was about 1961. We put up a garage first – I helped to shingle the roof, along with some of his archery buddies like Joe Davy, an electrician who also wired the place. Dad, Phil and I would go out there in winter and light a fire in the wood stove. Dad drew up some plans for a house and hired contractor Phil Lamb. I considered him an enemy, part of a conspiracy to take me away from my world, my friends. Worse, the new destination was decidedly rural.

McGregor was little more than a wide place in the road, though it did have a gas station, St. Clements Catholic church, a couple of stores, a hotel, a grain elevator, and a bowling alley with a pool room. The locals, for the most part, were the type Windsor people considered yokels and plowboys, the last thing any of us wanted to be. These were the people who drove cars with those goofy monkey's nuts dangling around the interior, and maybe stupid foam-rubber dice hanging from the mirror. I tried to put the best spin on it by saying the place was "just off Walker road," which it was, but you couldn't fool anybody. The only one from the old hood who respected the place, oddly enough, was Bob Kerr, who knew some of the people there, Leonard Meloche and those guys, though I don't know how, maybe through a relative. Yes, they dress like yokels, Bob would say, but they can handle themselves. This was true. A lot of these people were strong as oxes from farm work. But of course it didn't matter.

I was leaving, out of it, a centershot. My brothers Phil and Ralph, on the other hand, hadn't built up the support network I had and were eager to move. They even liked the idea of living in the country. This didn't help fraternal relations.

Dad took a leave of absence from his job and worked on the house. The cabinet guy set up his tools and built the units from scratch. All told, the project was quite an accomplishment. Later, when dad put up a shed, Jimmy Dugal came and helped. We had sunk in posts about a foot thick at the four corners and Jimmy climbed them like a logger, nailing on the joists. He always hit it off with my dad, who let Jimmy store some of his car parts on the property.

Meanwhile, the knowledge that we were "moving away," made it difficult for me. But I suppose the move took place at a natural breaking point. High school, after all, would change everything for everybody. Most would go to Massey, but not all. Some would opt for W.D. Lowe Technical school, known as "Tech," or Alicia Mason, a girl's vocational school.

The arrangement of elementary school, grades one through eight, then on to high school, is a good and natural one in my view. A separate "junior high" or "middle school" for grades six through nine or whatever strikes me as unnecessary, disruptive and wasteful. When I was in seventh grade it seemed to me, for the first time, that things were moving along rather swiftly. Wasn't it just the other day that John Tregaskiss and I showed up at Miss Bell's grade-one class? One more year and that would be it for old Glenwood, a school of Area A, Sandwich West Township.

In 1963, the last year for "Dobie Gillis" on television, the last day of school took on special meaning. I had been with some of these kids for the duration, eight years. That was a long time, a lot of marathon classes, many assemblies and many renditions of the school song. I had worked over a lot of fractions and common denominators. I had played countless games of football and "foot hockey," continued at recess. I had compared notes about what we had done over the summer or Christmas holiday. We all held a kind of seniority, a veteran status about to expire. Appropriately enough, I had actually moved from one end of the school to the other, with the grade-eight class at the opposite end from Miss Bell's. By then she was gone, and soon I would be too.

I wanted to be with these same kids in high school but that wasn't going to happen. Likewise, the teachers had been around for years, fixtures in our lives. They would stay while we all moved on.

My grade eight teacher was Mr. Hinch, whom I liked and respected. I learned a lot from him, and picked up his habit of saying "in a sense," when answering a question with some nuance. I remember him saying that the class had caused him go partially bald. I can believe it.

On that hectic last day, the time came to receive our diplomas. I was one of the first, which comes from having a last name beginning with "B." When I came up, Mr. Hinch said to me "watch your attitude."

That had a sting to it when I was expecting something nice, even some platitude about achievement, great things lying ahead. But old Hincho was absolutely right. I had an attitude all right, and I needed to watch it.

Many of us had talked about this day, acting as though we couldn't wait to get out. In my case anyway, liberation came with pangs of sadness.

No more pencils no more books, no more teacher's dirty looks. No more the smell of stale bread and peanut butter. No more rummaging in the "cloakroom," and no more writing "I will keep my boots in place" a hundred times. Yes, liberation from all that, but no more classmates, and no more predictable world. No more Paul MacKeegan, Sharon Kendall, Linda Gasparini, Bill Pengelly, John Tregaskiss, Linda Todd, Peter Faulkner, Jackie Wade, Gary Barker, Larry Roy, David Gourley, Ann Littlehales, and scores of others, every name with a face and stories behind it.

We spent the last day making noise and a great mess of the classroom. Some kids had bragged that on the last day they would smoke cigars in the hall or denounce the teachers and principal, but of course that never happened.

Ken Havens and some others had opted for Tech but most were going to Massey, which we could see out the window, and which we had seen rise from the ground. Some of us had floated rafts and skated on the excavation. Now came the stark reality that I was no longer part of that world. My brief shop classes with Mr. Bellaire would be all that I would ever see of the place. I was the one with the explaining to do, but I had little clue as to what awaited me in the world beyond south Windsor. All I really knew for certain was that it wasn't what I wanted. And you don't plan to get what you don't want. Then the bell rang, or maybe it would be better to say that the bell tolled. We spilled out in the school yard, said some final goodbyes and were gone. The eight-year run at Glenwood was over, and so was a defining span of our lives.

I walked down Norfolk to McKay as I had hundreds of times. This trip held a finality I could feel, even though the move would not come until

August. I would try and make the most of the time, and spend a lot of it with a girl I will call Cheryl.

She went to Central and I think we met at a dance. We had been an item for a while, to the point that some of my friends, Gord Cushman and Lyle Goulet cut me out of the loop because I spent so much time with her. We would linger in the park listening to the radio. "Our Day Will Come," by Ruby and the Romantics, got a lot of play. There was also a raucous instrumental called "Bust Out," by The Busters, a title Cheryl thought outrageous. I would go over to where she was babysitting, a common practice.

I remember hearing "Enamorado," this syrupy Spanish song that somehow made the charts. I guess I was rather *enamorado* at the time. I believe "Dominique" in French and "Sukiyaki," by Kyu Sakamoto, in Japanese, also charted that year. Another tune of the time "We're Only Young Once," by Bunny Paul, seemed to linger in my mind. It's true and I was living out my one chance. "Hey Girl," by Freddy Scott also got a lot of play. Like other tunes that summer, it was an appropriate sound track.

Cheryl was usually accompanied by Julie Matthews, who lived on her block of Virginia Park. Julie was younger and kind of a wannabe. Her brother Wayne failed ninth grade, maybe twice, and by one account stood up in class and announced he was going to fight and die for his country, then stomped out of the school and went off to join the Navy. Dave Drayton did likewise, and so did Wayne Pitre, the wiry little guy who drove a maroon Anglia. Some of the guys who joined the Navy had second thoughts. You joined for multiples of seven years, but could buy your way out.

Wayne Matthews should have become a race driver. He once had this 1952 Chevrolet and by gunning it in spurts could get the front wheels to come off the ground, a kind of second-hand wheelstand. He did this down by Shady's. When you went for a ride with Wayne Matthews, you didn't soon forget it.

The logical thing for Cheryl would have been to drop me since I was moving on. True, it wasn't far, but I wouldn't be driving for another two years, and it was too far for a bicycle, especially in winter. It might as well have been a move to Calgary or Vancouver. That would have been better, in fact, a cleaner break. Like Popeye in the Chubby Checker song, I would become a hitchhiker. I was a lame duck, but Cheryl stuck with me.

That summer the Reaumes were hosting parties at their house, evidently in the belief that it was better for the kids to carry on there than elsewhere. We played records and danced. Major Lance got a lot of play with his "Mickey's Monkey." You weren't supposed to "neck," but everybody did, especially Tom Hannan and Lynn Gatrall, who really got into it.

I hung around the Dairy Bar and Rak 'n Snak, saw what people I could, but now the leisurely pace of summer disappeared and the days seemed to fly by. Nobody held any formal going-away ceremonies, and I would not have wanted that in any case. Finally moving day arrived, hot and humid. I got up early and rode my bike around the usual circuit, Curry Park, St. Mary's Academy, Central Park, Woolco, the Dairy Bar. I should have gone by Shady's, the Devonshire pond and the rail yards, but time was limited. I also went by Glenwood, and the baseball diamonds at Christ the King, where Brian "Tiny Tears" Menard had pitched a ball over the backstop, and where I had hit home runs but where Gary Johnson also struck me out on three pitches. Success and failure, thrills and disappointments, trial and error, highs and lows. Even kids experience that.

Back at the house I helped load the stuff. Then I asked if I could say some goodbyes before we left. My parents said go ahead. Just as I had come to terms with the move, because I had to, in the closing days they now seemed to realize how much it would affect me. When the Lantzes and other neighbors came to say goodbye, my mom told them that we weren't going far and that, in fact, "we were just off Walker road," she said. This came as little comfort.

I went over to where Cheryl was babysitting, just a few blocks away. We didn't say much and there wasn't much time. I did, as Johnny Mathis said, get misty, and so did she. I don't think a song was playing at that moment because I would have remembered it, and I don't. Maybe our day would come, as Ruby and the Romantics said, if we just wait a while. But it didn't seem so at the time.

When I got back our first house was empty and somehow eerie. I walked through the place, remembering all that had gone on there, Christmas and birthdays, the arrival of Ralph, the bowling sessions in the hallway, ping-pong in the basement, my mother playing the piano. For the record, I wrote something in pencil on the back door jamb, about how the Billingsley family had lived in the place. Four of us came to this house, and now we were five. Seeing it empty again was indeed strange. Before long we were ready to go. We got into the 1959 Rambler station wagon and rolled out of the neighborhood as a family for the last time.

Hitchhike

The next time I talked to Cheryl, which wasn't long afterward, she said that she and Julie Matthews had gone over to our house later that night.

"It was all empty," she said. That swept the sadness back again. Meanwhile, I was dealing with the move as best I could. I had to ride a bus to Essex District High School, in the middle of the county. That made it hard to play sports or hang out with one's classmates.

The first two years were particularly difficult, though I did find reminders of the old hood from an old hobo type in McGregor named Bob Gesco. I once overheard him in a furious argument, during which he told someone to "make like the birds and *fuck off.*" He didn't quite have the nuances down.

Whenever possible, I would hitchhike into Windsor, where I would hang out as before and attend the Teentown dances at Southwood. On these hitchhiking trips, I came to realize how many people in Windsor knew my mother from her substitute teaching. As soon as I mentioned my last name they would make the connection. She made an impression on them all right.

Once into town, I would first go to the Rak to see if I could hook up with some friends. Some times this worked, sometimes it didn't. And sometimes I provided an occasion for improvisational comedy.

"Come to the party, Lloyd," Mark Lantz would say. "We're going to play pin the top on the silo." I was also invited to play "spin the pitchfork." When I told friends that my father had purchased a 1965 Chevrolet Impala, someone said "I thought he drove a tractor." I didn't like this at all but endured it. Better to be the butt of jokes than to be shunned. Everybody knew I didn't want to move.

I would go to the dance, just as before, but instead of a short walk home I would be out on Dougall or No. 3 Highway, freezing my skinny ass off, trying to get back home. That could take a few hours. I still wore a pair of those stupid moccasin things, the worst shoes you could wear in cold weather. But I kept them until they literally fell apart. Such was my desire to be in with the in crowd.

During these years we somehow managed to acquire beer and would stash it in snowdrifts on Roseland Golf Course. Then we would go out there later to drink and sing Motown songs, attempting all those moves that the Temptations used to make. It must have been quite a sight. Amazingly, we were never busted a single time.

My parents kept going to the Brookview club near River Canard, where some Windsor people could always be found, and where Murray Loomis was the lifeguard, he of the vaunted "fastest boots in Windsor," and a fan of Roy Orbison. Jim Ouellette also worked the pool. These were welcome links with the old days, but I didn't yet think of them that way.

When at last I could drive things became easier. I actually had a part-time job at Sentry, in the shoe department. There I was once rewarded $25 for catching a shoplifter. In 1966, the year Windsor annexed Sandwich West Township, I bought a motorcycle, one of those 250cc six-speed Suzukis that sounded like a sewing machine but could really fly. Chappy Bettany had a Yamaha 250, also a two-cycle engine, and we had some good drag races, fleeing from the cops on one occasion. Gord Cushman and Dwayne Pickle were at this time riding single-cylinder 350 Ducatis and Tom Ainsor had a white 160 Ducati. Tom Hannan, after going for a ride with me, thought my bike was swifter than the Ducati 350s. So did Tom "H.T." Ouellette, after trading me one night for his car, a green Studebaker, so I could go on a decent date. Tom put Danny Langlois on the back and they zoomed around town popping wheelies. H.T. was raving about the bike when he brought it back. I had put a different front sprocket on it, lowering the gear ratio, chromed the front fender and trimmed the rear one.

H.T. and I also made the trip to Toledo, where you could drink watered-down "3.2" beer at age 18. The hot place was the Peppermint Club, where the house band was The Raging Storms. They were pretty good on tunes like "Hang on Sloopy." There was even a poem going around:

Forty miles from Toledo, a short way to go
Where beer and whisky flows
Hello Toledo, hello rocks and rye
What do we give a shit if Windsor's gone dry?

Tom Ferri and I also made the trip. The girls in Toledo, we found, were very friendly. And as in "Surf City," it did seem there were two girls for every boy.

I think Mark Lantz was the first to make the jump to a larger motorcycle, a Triumph Bonneville, the machine of choice in Windsor. If I had bought one of those as my first bike I might well have wound up with a different crowd or, more likely, wrapped around a telephone pole.

I would ride the Suzuki to Point Pelee on Sundays, where the Windsor crowd would be out in force. I would also come in to Capri Pizza, next to the A&W on Dougall, on Saturday nights. The A&W didn't allow motorcycles but I drove in anyway. I sold the bike the next year, for a good price. At that time, four wheels were definitely better than two.

In the summers I worked at Stokeley's canning factory in Essex, then Green Giant in Harrow, where we had these great tomato fights on the night shift, and people would chuck bags of flour out of upper-story windows. The summer of 1967 it was Heinz in Leamington, where some Windsor people also worked, including Joe Primeau. We got some laughs at the expense of some of the rural types. There was this one guy from the sticks who talked like some pioneer. He didn't like the night shift. "My daddy says the day's for workin' and the night's for sleepin,'" he would remark. Primeau called him the "Cool duke of all time." One Arab worker who spoke no English and got dubbed Ahab, after the famous Ray Stevens song.

Rich Michalksi and some other friends also worked summers in Leamington, sleeping in laundromats and eating at Sue's Coffee Shop. At one time they were punching in at several places, spending the day at the beach, then punching out. They got away with it for a while.

By the end of my high school years I had made some friends out in the county and had a steady girlfriend I will call Jane. She was one reason why, by the time I finished high-school, I wanted to leave the entire area. While we were supposed to be an item, I found out she was going out on the side with members of the Queensmen. It was about that time I started getting into the blues.

John Tregaskiss visited his native England and brought back an album by Jimi Hendrix, then unavailable in the United States or Canada. We listened to it in wonder. We had never heard anybody quite like that. The Paul Butterfield Blues Band also turned us on to many of Hendrix's influences, the Chicago blues sound of Junior Wells, James Cotton, Buddy Guy and many others.

In the summer of 1967 I was driving a black-and-white 1956 Buick Century four-door hardtop I had bought from a friend for, yes, $35. You turned the key and started it by pushing the gas pedal to the floor. It burned oil and the idler arm was so worn that you could turn left by pushing the brake and taking your hands off the steering wheel. I sold it, paid off some debts, and left Heinz at the end of the summer season.

Others were starting college or working full-time in automobile factories. I turned 18 on September 19, and didn't know what I was going to do. But by this time I wanted to ship out. The move to the county, though involuntary, had broken my streak in town, as it were, and change was in the wind. The

Windsor scene by then seemed somehow stagnant, the sort of place you want to get away from.

That summer riots broke out in Detroit, some very rowdy stuff, with the "burn baby burn" crowd in ascendance, and troops in the streets. I watched the smoke rise from the Windsor waterfront, and that signaled an end to those quick trips through the tunnel we had taken for years without a second thought. It was best to avoid the place altogether, and my father had some difficulties getting to work. I had plenty of sympathy for the plight of black people in America but the riots didn't make me want to stay in the motor cities.

In *American Graffiti*, high on my list of favorite movies, and very similar to the scene in the motor cities, Wolf Man Jack tells Richard Dreyfuss that it's a great big beautiful world out there. No good reason to sit around sucking on popsicles. The intricacies of automobiles and drag racing no longer commanded my attention. The Lou Rawls tune "Dead End Street" began to take on a special meaning. The place I lived seemed like a dead end street. I too wanted to push my way out of there. I wanted to get out in the world and learn something, but maybe come back some day and straighten it all out. Perhaps this account will serve that purpose, at least in part.

In late summer, 1967, after the riots, I was sitting in the Dairy Bar, discussing the prospects of a move to Vancouver. I had read an article in *MacLean's,* to which my parents subscribed, titled, "Why Don't All Canadians Live in Vancouver?" It showed the city skyline, the beaches at Spanish Banks and English Bay, and a phalanx of pretty girls. This seemed like the place to go, but there might be a problem. The Windsor locals said it was hard to get a job there. Plus it rained a lot, which is true. Some, including Tom Dugal I believe, had gone out there, found no work, and come back in short order. At the time, this only made me more determined to go, and I did.

In mid-October, 1967, my father dropped me off at the waterfront in Detroit. As one who had moved about himself, he was officially okay with my plans, but it had to have hurt him to see his firstborn son move on. I took the bus to the airport then flew to Winnipeg, through Minneapolis, then took the train the rest of the way, seeing relatives on the way. When I woke up in the middle of the Rockies, the first mountains I had ever seen, it seemed clear I had done the right thing. I had grown up, after all, in a town where the highest point was a freeway overpass.

I got a job in Vancouver with little trouble, at a place called Coast Metals, down by Cambie and Broadway. The shop classes I had taken at Essex turned out to be useful. I could weld and braze, skills that kept me employed when others got laid off. The following March I was about to buy a 650 Triumph motorcycle, not a Bonneville but the single-carb model. I backed out of the deal. I was thinking of going to Australia, where jobs abounded, and employers would even pay your way. Instead I headed south for California, about as crazy a place in 1968 as has ever existed, and which saw me coming and swallowed me up. In California, as the Beatles said, the Magical Mystery Tour was waiting to take me away, and it did.

In the argot of the time, I turned on, tuned in, and dropped out. The following summer I was back in Vancouver, walking by English Bay blowing some blues on a harmonica, when John and Dave Tregaskiss drove by. It was the first of many reunions that have continued to this day. My adventures that particular day, and elsewhere, will have to be chronicled some other time.

For now, I will say that I spent some time in Big Sur, a pleasant place. I saw Jimi Hendrix live, on a bill with the Vanilla Fudge and the Soft Machine. Like Jake and Elwood Blues, I went on a mission from God. I have heard babies cry, and watched them grow. I have faced the dawn with sleepless eyes and watched many a sunset over the Pacific Ocean. As Hampton Hawes said, I have been shot at and missed but shit at and hit. I have met Mose Allison, Hank Crawford, Eddie Harris, Dave Brubeck, and David Newman, my favorite saxophonist. And Charlton Heston, whom I saw on the big screen in *Ben Hur*, gave me a cover endorsement for *Hollywood Party*, my book about the adventures of the studio Stalinists. I certainly did not foresee that, and a whole lot more, in 1959.

We're Only Young Once

After the events of September 11, 2001, crossing the border is no longer a simple matter. You now need passports, and even if everything is in order, they look you over pretty good, on both sides. In those conditions, few will simply slip over for a drink, or to buy shoes at Tom McCann's. And Hudson's is gone. Canadian adolescents have no incentive to seek a lower drinking age in Ohio, to go gambling in Las Vegas, or to see a show at the Empress Burlesque in Detroit, if that establishment still existed. Indeed, in highly technical language, Windsor is the naked dancing capital of Canada, and maybe the world, known far and wide for the "Windsor ballet." The "peelers," as locals call them, provide the benefit of hindsight. And foresight, for that matter. The dancing establishments, I suppose, are the modern equivalent of service stations.

Speaking of automotive, it's still a motor city, with mini-vans rolling off the line, but now a billboard reading WHAT CASINOS BUILD BUILDS WINDSOR would be appropriate. It is no longer possible for anybody gleefully to quit school in the belief that a high-paying, secure job is always available at Chrysler, Ford or General Motors. Those places aren't exactly hiring, and Windsor's unemployment rate is among the highest in Canada. Detroit also remains a motor city, but its decline is a matter of record, and evident to all but the willfully blind. Of the Big Three automakers Ford is performing the best, and Roy O'Brien Ford is still urging buyers to "stay on the right track, to Nine-Mile and Mack." Detroit and Windsor will remain linked in many ways. I hope I have provided some evidence for that reality, even as I chart some of the changes.

It's been some time since CKLW was the motor cities' heavyweight champ in radio. The decline likely began after the government imposed standards for Canadian content. It survived that but in the 1970s listeners started to tune in FM for music and abandon AM, which moved to news and talk. By the mid-1980s most of the CKLW DJs were gone, and so was Rosalie Trombley, everybody's favorite little record girl, as Bob Seger said. But she and the station had worked overtime as hitmakers and the fame of the artists endured. At one point the station adopted the "music of your life" format, but it had already played the music of our lives. You can find it, and some of the same DJs, on oldies stations, even if you have moved on to jazz, classical or whatever. When I hear Smokey Robinson and the Miracles singing "Going to a Go-Go," as I did just the other day, it still brings a response of delight. The motor city sound lives, but some things have an existential problem.

The *Sandwich West Herald* has disappeared and, as I discovered, none of the libraries has the back issues. That is a huge loss. Worse, the Tops Dairy Bar closed around 1971, an event that surely changed life for many. A Toronto Dominion Bank now occupies the site, and on one trip I exchanged some currency there, explaining to a friendly teller what the place used to be. She was interested, and so were some of her co-workers. You could sense some ghosts in the place, but there was no trace of the reeking potion Lyle Goulet once left near the fan. Acting on a tip from Ken Havens, who got me in trouble with his Chef Boy Ardee cartoon, I did chase down Pete, who used to work there.

He's now retired and works as a crossing guard at Southwood school. I showed up there one day and rattled off some names, Greg Templeton, John Varney, the Bertellis. Pete remembered them, and others, in considerable detail. Turns out that the Dairy Bar was his first job, in 1961, when he was 18 years old. That day I also glanced into the empty Southwood gym, which looked so very small. At the Teentown dances it had seemed a vast ballroom, a place where you might see a stranger, across the crowded room.

Fred Chalmers Service, the White Rose service station across the street, has also vanished, replaced by a convenience store. But Hank Villaincourt, the genial mechanic who patched many an inner tube, went on to work as a mechanic at Dan Kane Chevrolet, a dealership that did not exist in the old days.

St. Mary's Academy, it turned out, would not stand forever. Despite efforts to save it as an historic building, which it was, some developer, a wheeler-dealer type, bought the school and, in 1977, blew it up. This atrocity had the local talk shows buzzing. Someone said it was the only building for miles that had any class, not entirely true, but there was nothing like the place, maybe in the entire province. Jim Monforton, then in real estate, scored a publicity coup by buying the ornate tower. His smiling photograph appeared in the *Windsor Star*. I don't know what happened to the grotto, where we used to pour wax on our hands. I hope they reassembled it someplace, as they had done before. The grounds are now covered with houses. They called the development "St. Mary's Gate" and left a remnant of the Academy's gates standing, paltry and token evidence of what had stood there so majestically for decades. Take it or leave it, the place conveyed a sense of divine oversight and timeless tranquility that seems missing now.

The Grand Marais Ditch is now officially the Grand Marais Drain, banks all filled in with concrete and no natural gas pipe to cross. Ditch or drain, a lot of water has flowed down it since Little Richard, Elvis, and Chuck Berry were the favorites on the jukebox. The footbridge at the end of McKay is also long gone and the vacant lots have been filled with houses. Down the block, a garage stands beside the residence at 3116, our family's first house. Those are now going for $150,000 or so. The lawn looks fine but the elm tree in the back yard, where my father shot the starling with his bow and arrow, is gone, a victim of Dutch Elm disease. The sunburst locusts my parents planted are now gone, but they served their time with dignity. The last one survived until 2008.

Down at Glenwood, the weeping birch planted as part of an Arbor Day ceremony in front of Mr. Mansfield's class, is still doing well, a silent survivor along with some of the original bike racks. The big trees in the yard still stand as witnesses. So does the baseball backstop behind Christ the King school, though Christ the King church, like St. Mary's, has been demolished. It's foolish to believe that any city will not change over half a century, but one can't help but notice.

By the mid-70s Rak 'n Snak was gone, and with it the second most popular hangout, a natural meeting place, with plenty of parking, and very convenient to the beer store to boot. Various restaurants have occupied the property, but the Rak could never be replaced. John Dowhan, Mike Derbyshire, and the rest of the crowd had to find another venue for snooker.

Woolco became a Wal-Mart and looked basically the same. But you couldn't go in the record department and move around the letters on the top-ten list. And you won't see Rick Michalski running along the front of the store and crashing into the St. Vincent de Paul bin, or hiding inside it and terrifying passersby. And in the record department, where Michelle Reaume once worked, they don't carry any LPs by Chuck Berry, the Ventures or anybody else. In 2002 they demolished the whole building and build a new Wal-Mart at the north end of the parking lot. The little strip mall that was home to Rak 'n Snak remains, though for how long no one knows.

Capri Pizza moved to the other side of Dougall, but I doubt if Tony, who dubbed Jim Dugal "Gasoline," is still around. Leo Ferri gave up ownership of the Shell station long ago, and only Tom and Tony remain of the four brothers. Like many others, Tom has moved out to the county. As an adult, you can do that without fear of being mocked. If still there I would do the same.

Word is that Dickie is the last of the Bertelli brothers, so nobody will show up wanting to fight Leonard. But plenty of people in town still want to fight. The *Windsor Star* recently reported about a driver careening out of control down Walker Road, finally smashing into a wall. An off-duty cop was attending to the man when one of those he had cut off ran up and kicked him in the head. That's Windsor.

Apparently Dickie and Dave Tregaskiss are now friends, and have reviewed their past battles. Dave is in fantastic shape and looks like he would have little trouble taking down, say, Mike Tyson. He still rides motorcycles, but not a Norton Atlas. Those are hard to find now, and they want a lot of money for them. Same goes for old Triumphs. Harley-Davidson is now the *de rigueur* machine in Windsor.

The three Hi-Ho drive-in restaurants are long gone, along with the Top Hat, Riviera, and the Sandhill. The Three Bears is now a strip club. The Elmwood, where Sammy Davis Jr. and Jimmy Durante used to perform, is now some sort of detox center, which perhaps makes some sense. Bob-Lo also went through some changes.

Some baboons escaped from the zoo in 1972 and had to be retrieved from the fun house. They put in a big roller coaster in 1973. The clown Captain Bob-Lo retired in 1974, at 90, and died the next year. The place was sold to new owners in 1979 and things began to get rowdy on the boats and in the park. The Outlaws motorcycle gang busted up the place in 1987. The carousel was sold off in 1991 and the rest of the rides in 1994. The two Bob-Lo boats, the Columbia and St. Clair, built in 1902 and 1910 respectively, were auctioned off. Where they might be now I couldn't say, but probably in pieces. No more fun cruises down the Detroit River, trying to get the band to play "Tequila." An era had ended. Now the island is strictly residential.

By then the Nomads and Queensmen no longer had the territory to themselves. They had to vie with the Lobos and Satan's Choice, really nasty, violent gangs into drugs big-time. Those too have now given way. The Hell's Angels now have a clubhouse just outside of town.

A more significant milestone was the closing of the N&D around 1999. Now that was a real stunner. Just when you thought some things might never change. We saw that place grow from a glorified mom-and-pop joint to a full-service store, another natural meeting place. We used to return pop bottles there, and you don't forget something like that. I mean, this was where your food came from, and you even got S&M green stamps with it. The building now houses a second-hand store and flea market. Meanwhile, the branch of the Windsor library across Grand Marais bears the name of Budimir, after the enterprising brothers, Nick and Dan, who founded the N&D.

Freeway construction meant the end of Bozo Bush, doubtless lamented by Slingshot Louie and his gang. Ashton's Motel moved to Malden Road and survived for a time. I wonder what happened to that great pinball machine, where we racked up many a free game while surreptitiously peering at *Playboy*. Only a strip of Rankin Bush survives, what urban planners call a "green belt." Better than nothing. I have verified that traces of old tree forts survive, betrayed by short sections of two-by-fours nailed to the trunk to facilitate climbing. I doubt anyone is trying to blow them up, in the style of Lyle Goulet, but it is possible.

Luigi's Spaghetti House, which we somehow imagined was a "hoor house," may no longer be found on Huron Line. The Blue Bell Motel, where Ken Durocher wanted to fight the kid on the bus, got a fresh coat of paint, but now it too has been shut down.

Pat and Hank's Fish and Chips, where you could eat a lot of French fries for not much money, no longer occupies a spot across from Christ the King church. Neither does Wansbrough's Sport Shop, even though the owner, Frank Wansbrough, became mayor of Windsor. Master Cleaners, which used to sponsor a softball team, is still there, looking like it could use a good cleaning itself. Another survivor, just around the corner, is the South Windsor Barber Shop on Longfellow, where Leo Santamaria, the incumbent since about 1969, still presides. The rest of that little strip mall remains, with those old-style thin bricks. Doctor Munholland, our family doctor, had his office in that little complex, the one right on the corner. The shoemaker's shop has vanished.

Shady's is now an outlet of Mac's Milk, a chain with no personality whatsoever that sells milk in plastic bags, unheard of when we grew up. Back then they brought milk right to your house, as Bobby Lewis said, and even put it in the milk chute. So what's all this about progress? Right beside the former Shady's, Roseland Golf Course continues in business. Bob Baker, my classmate from Glenwood, used to be the groundskeeper at Roseland before moving to the new Seven Lakes. I saw him there and he told me that Mr. Fidler, the feisty little Glenwood teacher, occasionally played the course. Mr. Fidler has since passed away, I recently learned. In 1999, John Tregaskiss, Peter Faulkner and I had breakfast with Mr. Hinch at Roseland, not far from where he now lives. He showed great recall, but I didn't ask him about his weekend job at the beer store. For his part, he didn't ask if I had improved my attitude.

By one account, George White, our Glenwood classmate, still lives in the same house on Everts, just him and his dad. Not a very exciting life, to be sure, but there's something remarkable about it as a triumph of sheer staying power. Peter Faulkner also tracked down Bessie Zivanovich, Glenwood's star teacher. She didn't remember him or any of us by name but duly posed for a photo and didn't make him stay after four.

Glenwood no longer teems with kids as it did in our time but in other ways remains unchanged. The drinking fountains are the same units, with that chrome shield over the spout. The original bike racks were still there, remarkably enough. I didn't verify whether they had installed doors on the bathroom stalls but they likely had. I'm not politically correct, but in a new century no schoolboy should have to take a dump in plain view of his contemporaries.

Nobody gets the strap at Glenwood now because the Ontario government maintains a no-spanking policy. I don't recall if Bobby Kribs got the strap back in the day, but I do know he took a wrong turn. Kribs was a rather goofy kid and a poor student but seemingly harmless. In a photo of his fourth-grade class, he towers over the others. He left school early and did a stint in St. Thomas, a provincial mental facility, then moved to Toronto, where his height got him tagged "Stretcher." There he became a bouncer at something called the Charlie's Angels Body Rub, which was in fact a hoor house. In 1977, Kribs, Saul Betech and Josef Woods raped and murdered Emanuel Jaques, a 12-year-old shoeshine boy. The case shocked Toronto and the nation and recently resurfaced when Kribs attempted to gain parole. I haven't seen him for decades, and it is just an opinion, but I wouldn't let him out.

McKay, Curry, Dominion, Everts, all the streets seem empty, evidence that there has been no re-run of the baby boom of which were part. In our day, drivers would always have to slow down for street games. If they didn't they would get an earful. Looking at the streets now, it's not clear how behemoths like the 1957 DeSoto or 1959 Mercury managed to fit. Those cars are now classics, at least those that haven't rusted into powder.

Central Pool still operates, and a young lifeguard was once interested to hear from me how the place had been a kind of social center. What used to be the store, where Rick shocked Barb Bouffort with his dog-turd gag, is now some kind of storage space. Long lines and shifts are things of the past and, as I verified with approval in 2003, they no longer use chlorine. The water was pleasantly warm that day, but the pool and the park eerily quiet.

You no longer find groups of teenagers listening to "Our Day Will Come" on transistor radios and probing each other under the tree out past right field. The baseball diamonds remain but the dugouts that Lyle Goulet tried to blow up are gone. And of course there is no spectacular view of St. Mary's. The Central Park tennis courts are still there but Curry Park no longer features a rain shelter, site of many a mumblypeg game. On the other hand, now Ray Langlois won't try to slide off the roof and break both arms. The shelter's concrete foundation survived for years, but now that too is gone, and so is the drinking fountain, and the concrete block at the bottom so the smaller kids could step up.

I can't monitor the place, but I would be very surprised to see football games like the ones Dave Tregaskiss and the Morencies used to stage. When Dave would punt the ball, in that tight spiral I thought it might never come down. And I haven't seen Derek Bennett, the Stankos, or anyone like them, chipping golf balls. Windsor now abounds in golf courses, an unlikely sport for the climate.

All traces of the old Devonshire racetrack and pond have of course long since disappeared, covered by pavement and the Devonshire Mall. As Joni Mitchell said, they paved paradise and put up a parking lot. I wonder what happened to the raft those kids had put the outboard motor on that summer day so long ago. And when they drained the pond I'm sure they found some good stuff, including knives, fishing tackle, and money.

The Chrysler Corporation became Daimler Chrysler for a time, but what they build still builds Windsor. The "big house," as we called it, is still the place to work. They assemble the Chrysler mini-van there, which is why the town has been able to ride out some hard times. People now enjoy more than three television channels, but the cast of characters has changed.

After 13 years in Detroit, Soupy Sales moved on to national fame. He passed away at age 83 in October of 2009, evoking memories of White Fang, Black Tooth, Willie the Worm, and of course the famous pie in the face. Captain Jolly passed away in 1994, and many of the heroes and idols of our time are also gone: Maurice Richard, Mickey Mantle, Marilyn Monroe, Steve McQueen, Jackie Gleason, Ray Charles, Lou Rawls, Jackie Wilson, Elvis, several of the Four Tops, who used to play Windsor. Who knows where Nolan Strong might be, or Jamie Coe, crooner of "The Fool," or Edwin Starr, Agent Double-O Soul. I like to think they are working some bar or casino someplace, and still drawing income from royalties.

Some of those we watched on television have resurfaced in strange ways. Take Zelda Gilroy, from "The Many Loves of Dobie Gillis." Sheila James, who played Zelda, is the stage name of Sheila Kuehl. She finally got her man in the 1977 pilot *Whatever Happened to Dobie Gillis?* in which she played Dobie's wife. That was odd because in the 1980s Kuehl came out as a professional lesbian, went to Harvard Law School, and became a politically correct state senator in California, my home since 1977. I can testify that the former television actress has made great contributions to that state's bankrupt and ungovernable condition. Her rival for Dobie, Tuesday Weld, did not become an A-list star but did earn an Academy Award nomination for her role in *Looking for Mr. Goodbar.*

The observations about Sheila Kuehl may be a good sign. We used to direct most of our criticism at those older than ourselves, as in "Hey hey LBJ, how many kids did you kill today?" and "Never trust anyone over 30." Now in a new century it's more like, "punkass, get that skateboard out of my driveway," and "Turn your hat around, pull up your pants, and get a job."

Those older than ourselves should remain a target when they deserve it, even as we pay respect to those who earned it.

The great Gordie Howe is still alive, though the Olympia in Detroit, where he played hockey for so many years, is gone and so is Briggs Stadium. Little Richard and Chuck Berry are still belting it out. They outlasted many in the hood, who have been dropping off for some time. All booms fade and the baby boom is no exception.

Crossing the River

At the end of Ray Bradbury's *Fahrenheit 451*, the film version, an old man dies "as he thought he would," before the snows of winter fell. Back in the day few of us gave much consideration to the matter, but I'm sure some did not die as they thought they would.

Not long after we moved to the county Danny Napier passed away, something to do with drinking too much. It sounds like Danny was living every day as though it was his last, then one day he turned out to be right.

Drugs took a toll on others, like Dave Drayton, who not long ago called me from London where he had been sent for treatment. He was on the way out and he knew it, but in good spirits and eager to tie up a few loose ends. He identified the other player in the heist of old man Elder's Cadillac and verified that he did have his way with one particular girl in the neighborhood and that the experience was "so fine." On the other hand, Dave assured me that a different girl, the one of wild reputation, did not "take on" six guys in the baseball dugouts at Central Park. In fact Dave, supposedly the prime participant, said this storied event never took place.

I believed him, on all counts. The truth has a way emerging near the exit door.

In his final months, Dave renewed his friendship with Rick Michalski, his fellow stylist and choreographer of the DRD dance step. Then he quietly slipped away.

I wasn't able to compare notes with Anita Totten, Sue Phillips, Dave Ferri, Mike Ferri, Gordy Moore, Peter Stoddard, or Rick Stacey, all departed. On one trip I learned that Paul Schultz, the original Poopdeck Paul, had passed away. So has his son, who was married to Jane Bettany, sister of Ted and Chappy. When I saw Jane in 2003, she managed to recall that I had failed to ask her to a dance 40 years earlier in 1963. I didn't recall such negligence on my part but I took her word for it, glad to see that she moved on.

So had Cheryl, whom I tracked down with help from Ken Havens. We met at a Tim Horton's Donuts, which did not exist in our time but now seem to occupy every corner. Not all patrons will remember the chain's founder, Tim Horton, who played defense for the Toronto Maple Leafs in the 1950s and 1960s. Cheryl told me that one of my former girlfriends had started

132

acting strange, using drugs, and hanging around with nefarious motorcycle types. We took a quick spin around the places where, as Bunny Paul sang, we were only young, once. She was right. We only had one shot at youth.

Some years earlier I hooked up with Corrine Musgrave in Los Angeles. She was amazed to connect with someone from grade school, but we didn't get into why she had been called "Draino" at Glenwood school. By the 1980s she had become a high-profile music journalist, interviewing groups such as The Band.

I ran into Bernie Muntz, the bully fond of cramming snow into one's face, when I went to see Jane, my high-school girlfriend, who was living in a ramshackle place on Howard. He was in some kind of motorcycle gang and while I was there he told Jane to put on the colors and go scare the neighbors. I didn't stay long.

Jim Dugal, who no longer stutters but has put on a lot of weight, bought a place on Everts, near Tecumseh, and can still be found building custom cars. It was Jimmy whose awesome mechanical gifts proved the most suitable for the motor city. I last saw Jim in July of 2009, and at first he didn't remember me. But that sign of decline did not prevent him from working away on a 1937 Ford, his latest masterpiece.

My friend Jim Ouellette, also known as "J-Dubs," still sold cars in Windsor, part of a family tradition, before heading west. His father Harry, who found the advent of Toyotas such a joke, passed away. JW found his father's old 1959 Ford in a junkyard and duly restored it, complete with two-tone green-and-white paint job, continental kit, and eight-track tape player. In 1993, we tooled around town in it. JW was then living near Southwood school, site of the famed Teentown dances, and where I played basketball with Pete McNab, not far from his old place on Mt. Royal, near Cousineau Rd. Older brother Tom briefly came back to town, where Danny Langlois remains, spending summers on his cabin cruiser. When I saw him there not long ago he verified the story of the failed pickup attempt in his red 1961 Ford convertible.

On Tecumseh, not far from Jim's Dugal's place, stands the new Nantais Sport Shop, still pronounced Naughtiss, and whose employees include my Glenwood schoolmates Bill Pengelly and Tom Jones. Pete Jones, the eldest of the three brothers, now lives in Pennsylvania. Bob is a construction superintendent living in northern California, not far from me, and visited me late in 2000.

We got caught up without talking about the fight we had over by the mulberry tree. I can't even remember what it was about, probably nothing. Like me, Bob Jones still visits his mother, who lives in Tecumseh. Bob told me Mrs. Timchyshyn, now well into her emeritus years, still lives on McKay in the same house. I don't know where Danny is now, but I heard from him not long ago. I bet he can still play pool with the best of them.

Glenn Brandt became an excellent drummer and his group, formerly Cross-Eyed Cats, are still rocking the Windsor scene, touring around the province, and making CDs. They once played gigs in Europe, backing Johnny Johnson, Chuck Berry's piano player. I bring my saxophone and sit it with them at the Canusa and other joints, most recently at a jam session at Dominion Golf Course. The people in the crowd have no clue what a momentous event that is for me. Maybe it's not straightening it all out, as Lou Rawls said, but it sure comes close. The current crowd will never see a rock-and-roll band playing on the roof of the concession stand at the Windsor Drive-in, now demolished. They'll never be under a spell, like a man in a well.

Where he may be now I couldn't say but in the mid-1970s, Johnny Spears was sighted retrieving shopping carts in the K-Mart parking lot on Huron Line. So the mercurial Johnny at least remained productive. Likewise Bob Ballance, in my class for most of the Glenwood years, is now a prominent attorney in town. Like others, he doesn't want to talk about the old days and I have no problem with that. Bob's older sister Judy showed me how to do the "Bristol Stomp" in the living room of their tri-level house on Mark Avenue.

The Tregaskiss brothers built the W. Tregaskiss company, not far from Cowpaddy Lake, into an international player by manufacturing the best welding equipment in the world. John lived for a time lived in Barbados, and now has a place in Windsor, along with Clive and Dave. Dave and Cheyenne, the former Nomad, ride their motorcycles to the famous gathering at Sturgis.

Bob Fox, stepson of our minister, spent a few years in Australia and now lives on Denman Island, British Colombia, making a living at various jobs, photographer, paramedic, lumber trader. He's got the remnants of an old Triumph Bonneville someplace, just as remnants of his old 500 Matchless were scattered around my dad's place.

Rick Michalski, a fine artist and capable musician, lived for years in Vancouver, in one of the last vestiges of the old Kitsilano culture, a drafty apartment above a Chinese restaurant. Rags was a holdout with a converted school bus and Volkswagen van surrounded by BMW driving yuppies in upscale condos. John Tregaskiss, Alan Farrell, Stu Heydon, myself and some other people made it there in March, 1997, for Rags' fiftieth birthday. We jammed and partied till the cows came home. Now Rags is back in Windsor, taking care of his mother and I recently saw him at a jam session. He remains a master of improvisational comedy, and told me a funny story about meeting Donovan the crooner of "Hurdy Gurdy Man." Rags greeted him as "Donnie."

Lyle Goulet, the chemistry-set joker who wanted to be called "Rocky," is also back in town, after stints at jobs including a nuclear power plant. I tracked him down in 2003, when he was living in a basement apartment near the welfare office. The years had not been kind to him. He looked wizened and frail, with patches of discolored skin. Gone was the look of mischievous glee. Lyle recalled some episodes from the old days but apocalyptic scenarios were his theme of choice. After about 15 minutes he walked off and I haven't seen him since.

Peter Faulkner, who should be Windsor's official historian, is a writer based in Calgary but makes a yearly trek to Windsor, where he goes to open houses in the old neighborhood and chases down old friends. Michael Bull, my fellow Glenwood projectionist, teaches sociology at Flinders University in Melbourne, Australia. He recently visited Glenwood school, where the principal remembered other graduates who had done the same thing.

Some of us in the diaspora may be doing better careerwise than we would have in Windsor, but we have paid a price. The small band that stayed, though they may not think about it, have suffered no disconnect from their roots. In an ever-shifting age that counts for something.

Some of those who sang the soundtrack to our lives have surfaced in strange ways. John Tregaskiss happened to be visiting his wife in a medical facility in Detroit. She introduced him to an aging black man, an orderly, who mentioned that he had once been in a musical group, but said that John had probably never heard of it. John asked for the group's name.

"The Contours," he said.

John promptly recited the opening lines of "Do You Love Me?" the best tune to shake 'em down at Teentown. The former Contour listened in wonder and even got misty over it.

Around the same time, John was visiting someone at a nursing home out by Cottam. There a man in a wheelchair looked somehow familiar. It turned out to be Tommy Durocher, the retarded kid from the big house on Curry near the Grand Marais Ditch, where I fell out of the tree and broke my arm. The two neighbors renewed their acquaintance. I truly believe the meetings could not have happened by pure chance.

Tommy Durocher passed away a few years ago and his photo in the *Windsor Star* obituary showed that same expression so familiar around Curry Park so long ago. Tommy Durocher attained the age of 60. Damn right he did.

My brother Phil, born in Detroit, who proudly said "that's my brother" at school and tried to follow me everywhere, duly became the best athlete of the family. I believe he could have played baseball or basketball at the professional level but he didn't get the chance to show what he could do. Phillip Hugh Billingsley died in 1977 of Hodgkins disease. He breathed his last at Grace Hospital. A tree has been planted in his memory at Victoria Memorial Gardens

Ten years later, in the winter of 1987, I visited my father, Kenneth Billingsley, in the same hospital. One of his lungs had collapsed. He battled emphysema and since his Merchant Marine days had had trouble breathing, compounded by heavy smoking, and it was starting to affect his heart. That day he looked well and we hung out as long as they would allow. I clung to him the way I had as a child. I tried to get his long-term prospects but the doctor had departed. It turned out that my father had run out of long-term prospects.

The tall Merchant Marine veteran who bought his first home on McKay Avenue in Windsor, who knew all my friends and played hide-and-seek with us, passed away suddenly in August of 1987. He was 63 years old. I arrived as fast as I could, thinking about how he seemed so larger than life. All those days fishing on the river came back, a tide of memories. Some of his work colleagues showed up at the memorial service. One found out I was his son and said to me, "I really loved Ken." A lot of people did. John Tregaskiss and his wife Kathy were also there. That meant more to me than I can say.

At the house, beside dad's favorite chair, lay the last book he had been reading. *Wild Goose Jack* is the autobiography of Jack Miner, the conservationist who had founded the bird sanctuary where my father would take us to watch the geese. Back in the day, Miner would tag the birds with biblical verses such as "with God all things are possible." I like to think that book helped prepare my father for his own final flight to a better place.

My brother Ralph and his family live in the house my father built in McGregor. Ralph stands as tall as our father, so a big man still bestrides the place, where our mother lives in a flat at the back. The studious woman who taught all my friends and told me that rock and roll was "strident and cacophonous" is still going strong in her late 80s. After all these years, she is still reading Shakespeare, playing the piano, and taking long walks in the country, observing the birds and beasts of the realm.

"You crazy kid," she said when I tried to cross the pipe over the Grand Marais Ditch. Maybe I'm still crazy after all these years, as Paul Simon said. Maybe, like Ray Charles, I'm just living a life of dreams of yesterday. Maybe so. Hardly a day goes by I don't think of the old days in the motor cities, for good reason.

"We laughed louder then," John told me not long ago. I think that is true.

Those days have laughed and run away, like a child at play, as Johnny Mercer wrote, but as long as anybody from that time remains I will never feel myself an orphan in this world, where none of us is a permanent resident. The Detroit River will keep rolling along, but we will all cross the river some day. Will there be a reunion at that big Dairy Bar in the sky? Or maybe a celestial Curry Park? I like to think so. We have lots to talk about.

In the meantime, those were the days my friends. We thought they would never end. But in a way they haven't ended, as long as we can think about them, talk about them, and write about them. I will do so as long as I live.

And I say to myself, it was a wonderful world. Yes, I had been there before, and I knew all about it. I remember, I remember. I'm still humming some song from 1962. It's been so long now, but it seems like it was only yesterday.

Lightning Source UK Ltd.
Milton Keynes UK
UKOW06f0122051117
312148UK00004B/270/P